Hands-On Kubernetes on Azure

Run your applications securely and at scale on the most widely adopted orchestration platform

Shivakumar Gopalakrishnan
Gunther Lenz

BIRMINGHAM - MUMBAI

Hands-On Kubernetes on Azure

Commissioning Editor: Vijin Boricha
Acquisition Editor: Shrilekha Inani
Content Development Editor: Nithin George Varghese
Technical Editor: Prashant Chaudhari
Copy Editor: Safis Editing
Project Coordinator: Drashti Panchal
Proofreader: Safis Editing
Indexer: Pratik Shirodkar
Graphics: Tom Scaria
Production Coordinator: Nilesh Mohite

First published: March 2019

Production reference: 1290319

Published by Packt Publishing Ltd.
Livery Place
35 Livery Street
Birmingham
B3 2PB, UK.

ISBN 978-1-78953-610-2

www.packtpub.com

I dedicate this book to my parents. Without their support on everything from getting my first computer to encouraging me on whatever path I took, this book wouldn't have happened.

-Shivakumar Gopalakrishnan

To Okson and Hugo

To everyone reading this

– Gunther Lenz

`mapt.io`

Mapt is an online digital library that gives you full access to over 5,000 books and videos, as well as industry leading tools to help you plan your personal development and advance your career. For more information, please visit our website.

Why subscribe?

- Spend less time learning and more time coding with practical eBooks and Videos from over 4,000 industry professionals

- Improve your learning with Skill Plans built especially for you

- Get a free eBook or video every month

- Mapt is fully searchable

- Copy and paste, print, and bookmark content

Packt.com

Did you know that Packt offers eBook versions of every book published, with PDF and ePub files available? You can upgrade to the eBook version at `www.packt.com` and as a print book customer, you are entitled to a discount on the eBook copy. Get in touch with us at `customercare@packtpub.com` for more details.

At `www.packt.com`, you can also read a collection of free technical articles, sign up for a range of free newsletters, and receive exclusive discounts and offers on Packt books and eBooks.

Contributors

About the authors

Shivakumar Gopalakrishnan is a DevOps architect at Varian Medical Systems. He has introduced Docker, Kubernetes, and other cloud-native tools to Varian's product development work to enable an everything-as-code approach. He is highly experienced in software development in a variety of fields, including networking, storage, medical imaging, and DevOps. He has developed scalable storage appliances for medical imaging needs and helped architect cloud ease solutions. He has enabled teams in large, highly regulated medical enterprises to adopt modern Agile/DevOps methodologies. He holds a Bachelor's degree in engineering from the College of Engineering, Guindy, and a Master's degree in science from the University of Maryland, College Park.

Thanks to all in the open source movement who constantly "chop wood and carry water". This book would not be possible without leveraging open source frameworks, samples, and documentation.

Thank you to my wonderful wife Asha, who took care of everything else so that I could focus on this book.

Thanks to Nikhil and Adil for helping me in all the ways that they could, including listening to me rambling about Config maps and Ingress.

Gunther Lenz is the Senior Director of the Technology Office at Varian. He is an innovative software research and development leader, an architect, an MBA graduate, a published author, a public speaker, and a strategic tech visionary with over 20 years' experience.

He has successfully led large, innovative, and transformational software development and DevOps teams of 50+ members. He has defined and led teams throughout the entire software product life cycle using ground-breaking processes, tools, and technologies. He was a Microsoft Most Valuable Professional for Software Architecture (one of the only 180 globally) from 2005 to 2008. Gunther has published two books: .NET-A Complete Development Cycle and Practical Software Factories in .NET.

About the reviewer

Kapil Bansal is a technical consultant at HCL Technologies in India. He has more than eleven years of experience in the IT industry. He has worked on Microsoft Azure (PaaS, IaaS, Kubernetes, and DevOps), ALM, ITIL, and Six Sigma. He provides technical supervision and guidance during clients' engagement execution. His expertise includes strategic design and architectural mentorship, assessments, POCs, sales life cycles, consulting on engagement processes, and so on. He has worked with companies such as IBM India Pvt Ltd., NIIT Technologies, Encore Capital Group, and Xavient Software Solutions, and he has served clients based in the United States, the United Kingdom, India, and Africa, including T-Mobile, WBMI, Encore Capital, and Airtel.

Packt is searching for authors like you

If you're interested in becoming an author for Packt, please visit `authors.packtpub.com` and apply today. We have worked with thousands of developers and tech professionals, just like you, to help them share their insight with the global tech community. You can make a general application, apply for a specific hot topic that we are recruiting an author for, or submit your own idea.

Table of Contents

Preface

Microsoft is now one of the most significant contributors to Kubernetes open source projects. Kubernetes helps to create, configure, and manage a cluster of virtual machines that are preconfigured to run containerized applications.

This book will you to monitor applications and cluster services to achieve high availability and dynamic scalability, to deploy web applications securely in Microsoft Azure with Docker containers. You will enhance your knowledge about Microsoft Azure Kubernetes Service and will learn advanced techniques such as solution orchestration, secret management, best practices, and configuration management for complex software deployments.

Who this book is for

If you're a cloud engineer, cloud solution provider, sysadmin, site reliability engineer, or a developer interested in DevOps, and are looking for an extensive guide to running Kubernetes in the Azure environment, then this book is for you.

What this book covers

Chapter 1, *Introduction to Docker and Kubernetes*, covers the concepts of Docker and Kubernetes, providing the foundational context for the following chapters, where you will dive into how to deploy Dockerized applications in Microsoft AKS.

Chapter 2, *Kubernetes on Azure (AKS)*, is a step-by-step instructional chapter on how to navigate the Azure portal to perform all the functions required to launch an AKS cluster, and also use Azure Cloud Shell without installing anything on your computer.

Chapter 3, *Application Deployment on AKS*, looks at the details of deploying an application on AKS, thereby teaching you about the usefulness of various Kubernetes concepts, such as pods, replication controllers, services, config maps, namespaces, and deployments.

Chapter 4, *Scaling Your Application to Thousands of Deployments*, shows how to scale deployments with Kubernetes by not only showing how to create multiple instances of the software, but also how to debug problems that you might run into.

Chapter 5, *Single Sign-On with Azure AD*, covers how to secure applications on an enterprise scale. By integrating applications with Azure Active Directory, readers can enable any application to link to an organization's Active Directory.

Chapter 6, *Monitoring the AKS Cluster and the Application*, will enable you to set alerts on any metric that you would like to be notified of by leveraging Azure Insights.

Chapter 7, *Operation and Maintenance of AKS Applications*, covers how to secure your AKS cluster with role-based security by leveraging Azure Active Directory as the authentication provider.

Chapter 8, *Connecting an App to an Azure Database - Authorization*, focuses on working with the WordPress sample solution, which leverages a MySQL database as a data store.

Chapter 9, *Connecting to Other Azure Services (Event Hubs)*, covers how to implement microservices on AKS, including how to use Event Hubs for loosely coupled integration between applications.

Chapter 10, *Securing AKS Network Connections*, explores Kubernetes secrets in more depth, covering different secrets' backends and how to use them. A brief introduction to service mesh concepts will also be covered with the implementation of a practical example.

Chapter 11, *Serverless Functions*, teaches you how to deploy serverless functions on AKS directly using Kubeless, if the requirement is to provide serverless functions within your organization network. You will also integrate AKS-deployed applications with Azure Event Hubs.

Chapter 12, *Next Steps*, will direct you to different resources where they can learn and implement advanced features in security, scalability. For this chapter, please refer to: https://www.packtpub.com/sites/default/files/downloads/Next_Steps.pdf

To get the most out of this book

Though any previous knowledge of Kubernetes is not expected, some experience with Linux and Docker containers would be beneficial.

Download the example code files

You can download the example code files for this book from your account at www.packt.com. If you purchased this book elsewhere, you can visit www.packt.com/support and register to have the files emailed directly to you.

You can download the code files by following these steps:

1. Log in or register at www.packt.com.
2. Select the **SUPPORT** tab.
3. Click on **Code Downloads & Errata**.
4. Enter the name of the book in the **Search** box and follow the onscreen instructions.

Once the file is downloaded, please make sure that you unzip or extract the folder using the latest version of:

- WinRAR/7-Zip for Windows
- Zipeg/iZip/UnRarX for Mac
- 7-Zip/PeaZip for Linux

The code bundle for the book is also hosted on GitHub at https://github.com/PacktPublishing/Hands-On-Kubernetes-on-Azure. In case there's an update to the code, it will be updated on the existing GitHub repository.

We also have other code bundles from our rich catalog of books and videos available at https://github.com/PacktPublishing/. Check them out!

Conventions used

There are a number of text conventions used throughout this book.

CodeInText: Indicates code words in text, database table names, folder names, filenames, file extensions, pathnames, dummy URLs, user input, and Twitter handles. Here is an example: "Mount the downloaded WebStorm-10*.dmg disk image file as another disk in your system."

A block of code is set as follows:

```
static const char *TAG="SMARTMOBILE";
static EventGroupHandle_t wifi_event_group;
static const int CONNECTED_BIT = BIT0;
```

When we wish to draw your attention to a particular part of a code block, the relevant lines or items are set in bold:

```
static const char *TAG="SMARTMOBILE";
static EventGroupHandle_t wifi_event_group;
static const int CONNECTED_BIT = BIT0;
```

Any command-line input or output is written as follows:

```
$ mkdir css
$ cd css
```

Bold: Indicates a new term, an important word, or words that you see onscreen. For example, words in menus or dialog boxes appear in the text like this. Here is an example: "Select **System info** from the **Administration** panel."

 Warnings or important notes appear like this.

 Tips and tricks appear like this.

Get in touch

Feedback from our readers is always welcome.

General feedback: If you have questions about any aspect of this book, mention the book title in the subject of your message and email us at customercare@packtpub.com.

Errata: Although we have taken every care to ensure the accuracy of our content, mistakes do happen. If you have found a mistake in this book, we would be grateful if you would report this to us. Please visit www.packt.com/submit-errata, selecting your book, clicking on the Errata Submission Form link, and entering the details.

Piracy: If you come across any illegal copies of our works in any form on the Internet, we would be grateful if you would provide us with the location address or website name. Please contact us at copyright@packt.com with a link to the material.

If you are interested in becoming an author: If there is a topic that you have expertise in and you are interested in either writing or contributing to a book, please visit authors.packtpub.com.

Reviews

Please leave a review. Once you have read and used this book, why not leave a review on the site that you purchased it from? Potential readers can then see and use your unbiased opinion to make purchase decisions, we at Packt can understand what you think about our products, and our authors can see your feedback on their book. Thank you!

For more information about Packt, please visit `packt.com`.

Section 1: The Basics

Section 1 of the book focuses on establishing the baseline and explaining the basic concepts necessary to build the foundational knowledge that the reader will require in order to follow the examples in the book. We not only want to make sure that the reader understands the basics of the underlying concepts, such as Docker and Kubernetes, but also that they are knowledgeable regarding the tools that they can use, such as Visual Studio, Visual Studio Code, and Cloud Shell.

The following chapters will be covered in this section:

- Chapter 1, *Introduction to Docker and Kubernetes*
- Chapter 2, *Kubernetes on Azure (AKS)*

1
Introduction to Docker and Kubernetes

The perfect storm – that is how the current state of the software development world can be described. The sources of this storm are as follows:

- **Open source software (OSS)**: This provides a foundational framework that makes almost any software possible.
- **Technology and architecture advancements**: This enables the orchestration of loosely coupled systems that consist of micro applications leveraging microservices, micro frontends, and multiple databases.
- **Public clouds**: For instance, Azure, AWS, and Google Cloud – these provide scalable infrastructure for a company of any size.
- **Containerization and orchestration**: For instance, Docker and Kubernetes – making DevOps culture possible.

Azure Kubernetes Service (AKS) packages and manages the complexity of putting together all of the preceding sources for you. As an engineer, it is still very useful to know the underpinnings of AKS technologies. We will explore the foundations of the technologies (you might be surprised to see how really *old* they are) that power AKS. You will learn about processes in Linux, and how Linux is related to Docker. Even though Kubernetes is technically a container runtime-agnostic platform (you will find out what this means shortly), Docker is the de facto container technology that is used practically everywhere. You will see how various processes fit nicely into Docker, and how Docker fits nicely into Kubernetes (just like the cute Russian dolls).

This chapter is the longest chapter that you will read in terms of theory in this book. You will get your hands dirty pretty quickly in the following chapters. Step by step, you will be building applications that can scale and are secure. This chapter gives you a brief introduction to the information that you will need if you want to dig deeper, or wish to troubleshoot when something goes wrong (remember, Murphy was an optimist!). Having cursory knowledge of this chapter will demystify much of the magic as you build your Azure AD-authenticated, Let's Encrypt-protected application that scales on demand based on the metrics that you are monitoring.

The following topics will be covered in this chapter:

- The foundational technologies that enable AKS
- The fundamentals of Docker
- The fundamentals of Kubernetes

Technical requirements

You will need a modern web browser, such as Chrome, Firefox, or Edge, for this chapter.

The foundational technologies that enable AKS

The combination of OSS, public cloud, and containerization gives a developer a virtually unlimited number of compute power combined with the ability of rapidly composing applications that deliver more than the sum of the individual parts. The individual parts that make up an application generally do only one thing, and do it well (take, for instance, the Unix philosophy).

The developer is now able to architect applications that are deployed as microservices. When done right, microservices, such as SOA, enable quick feedback during development, testing, and deployment. Microservices are not a free lunch and has various problems, which are listed in the 2014 article—*Microservices - Not A Free Lunch!* (you can read this article at `http://highscalability.com/blog/2014/4/8/microservices-not-a-free-lunch.html`). With the technologies we listed earlier, developers have the power of having their cake and eating it too, as more and more of the *not free lunch* part is available as managed services, such as AKS. The public cloud providers are competing by investing in managed services to become the go-to provider for developers.

You build it, you run it

Even with more managed services coming to relieve the burden on the developer and operator, developers need to know the underlying workings of these services to make effective use of them in production. Just as developers write automated tests, future developers will be expected to know how their application can be delivered quickly and reliably to the customer.

Operators will take the hints from the developer specs and deliver them a stable system – whose metrics can be used for future software development, thus completing the virtuous cycle.

Developers owning the responsibility of running the software that they develop instead of throwing it over the wall for operations is a change in mindset that has origins in Amazon (`https://www.slideshare.net/ufried/the-truth-about-you-build-it-you-run-it`).

The advantages of the DevOps model not only change the responsibilities of the operations and development teams—it also changes the business side of organizations. The foundation of DevOps can enable businesses to accelerate the time to market significantly if combined with a lean and agile process and operations model.

Everything is a file

Microservices, Docker, and Kubernetes can get quickly overwhelming for anyone. We can make it easier for ourselves by understanding the basics. It would be an understatement to say that understanding the fundamentals is critical to performing root cause analysis on production problems.

Any application is ultimately a process that is running on an **operating system (OS)**. The process requires the following to be usable:

- Compute (CPU)
- Memory (RAM)
- Storage (disk)
- Network (NIC)

Launch the online Linux Terminal emulator at `https://bellard.org/jslinux/vm.html?url=https://bellard.org/jslinux/buildroot-x86.cfg`. Then, type the `ls` command, as follows:

```
[root@localhost ~]# ls
dos         hello.c
[root@localhost ~]#
```

This command lists the files in the current directory (which happens to be the root user's home directory).

Congratulations, you have launched your first container!

Well, obviously, this is not really the case. In principle, there is no difference between the command you ran versus launching a container.

So, what is the difference between the two? The clue lies in the word, `contain`. The `ls` process has very limited containment (it is limited only by the rights that the user has). `ls` can potentially see all files, has access to all the memory, network, and the CPU that's available to the OS.

A container is **contained** by the OS by controlling access to computing, memory, storage, and network. Each container runs in its own **namespace**(`https://medium.com/@teddyking/linux-namespaces-850489d3ccf`). The rights of the namespace processes are controlled by **control groups (cgroups)**.

Every container process has contained access via `cgroups` and namespaces, which makes it look (from the container process perspective) as if it is running as a complete instance of an OS. This means that it appears to have its own root filesystem, init process (PID 1), memory, compute, and network.

Since running containers is just a set of processes, it makes it extremely lightweight and fast, and all the tools that is used to debug and monitor processes can be used out of the box.

You can play with Docker by creating a free Docker Hub account at Docker Hub (`https://hub.docker.com/`) and using that login at play with Docker (`https://labs.play-with-docker.com/`).

First, type `docker run -it ubuntu`. After a short period of time, you will get a prompt such as `root@<randomhexnumber>:/#`. Next, type `exit`, and run the `docker run -it ubuntu` command again. You will notice that it is super fast! Even though you have launched a completely new instance of **Ubuntu** (on a host that is probably running **alpine** OS), it is available instantly. This magic is, of course, due to the fact that containers are nothing but regular processes on the OS. Finally, type `exit` to complete this exercise. The full interaction of the session on play with Docker (`https://labs.play-with-docker.com/`) is shown in the following script for your reference. It demonstrates the commands and their output:

```
docker run -it ubuntu # runs the standard ubuntu linux distribution as a
container

exit # the above command after pulling it from dockerhub will put you into
the shell of the container. exit command gets you out of the container

docker run -it ubuntu # running it again shows you how fast launching a
container is. (Compare it to launching a full blown Virtual Machine (VM),
booting a computer)

exit # same as above, gets you out of the container
```

The following content displays the output that is produced after implementing the preceding commands:

```
##############################################################
#                        WARNING!!!!                         #
# This is a sandbox environment. Using personal credentials  #
# is HIGHLY! discouraged. Any consequences of doing so are   #
# completely the user's responsibilites.                     #
#                                                            #
# The PWD team.                                               #
##############################################################
[node1] (local) root@192.168.0.18 ~
$ docker ps
CONTAINER ID        IMAGE               COMMAND             CREATED
STATUS              PORTS               NAMES
[node1] (local) root@192.168.0.18 ~
$ date
Mon Oct 29 05:58:25 UTC 2018
[node1] (local) root@192.168.0.18 ~
$ docker run -it ubuntu
Unable to find image 'ubuntu:latest' locally
latest: Pulling from library/ubuntu
473ede7ed136: Pull complete
c46b5fa4d940: Pull complete
```

```
93ae3df89c92: Pull complete
6b1eed27cade: Pull complete
Digest:
sha256:29934af957c53004d7fb6340139880d23fb1952505a15d69a03af0d1418878cb
Status: Downloaded newer image for ubuntu:latest
root@03c373cb2eb8:/# exit
exit
[node1] (local) root@192.168.0.18 ~
$ date
Mon Oct 29 05:58:41 UTC 2018
[node1] (local) root@192.168.0.18 ~
$ docker run -it ubuntu
root@4774cbe26ad7:/# exit
exit
[node1] (local) root@192.168.0.18 ~
$ date
Mon Oct 29 05:58:52 UTC 2018
[node1] (local) root@192.168.0.18 ~
```

Orchestration

An individual can rarely perform useful work alone; teams that communicate securely and well can generally accomplish more.

Just like people, containers need to talk to each other and they need help in organizing their work. This activity is called orchestration.

The current leading orchestration framework is Kubernetes (https://kubernetes.io/). Kubernetes was inspired by the Borg project in Google, which, by itself, was running millions of containers in production. Incidentally, cgroups' initial contribution came from Google developers.

Kubernetes takes the declarative approach to orchestration; that is, you specify what you need and Kubernetes takes care of the rest.

Underlying all this magic, Kubernetes still launches the Docker containers, like you did previously. The extra work involves details such as networking, attaching persistent storage, handling the container, and host failures.

Remember, everything is a process!

Summary

In this chapter, we introduced the concepts of Docker and Kubernetes. This provides the common context for the following chapters, where we will dive into how to deploy Dockerized applications in Microsoft AKS. You will see how the AKS PaaS offering from Microsoft streamlines deployment by taking on many of the management and operational tasks that you may have to do yourself if you manage and operate the Kubernetes infrastructure.

In the next chapter, we will introduce the Azure Portal and its components in the context of managing AKS.

Kubernetes on Azure (AKS) 2

Installing and maintaining Kubernetes clusters correctly and securely is hard. Thankfully, all the major cloud providers such as **Google Cloud Platform** (**GCP**) (of course, considering Kubernetes was founded in Google), AWS, and Azure facilitate installing and maintaining clusters. You will learn how to navigate through Azure Portal and launch your own cluster and a sample application. And all of the above from your browser.

The following topics will be covered in this chapter:

- Navigating Azure Portal
- Launching your cluster
- Starting your first application

Technical requirements

You will need a modern web browser such as Firefox, Chrome, Safari, or Edge.

If you do not have an Azure account, you can create a free account here: `https://azure.microsoft.com/en-us/free/?WT.mc_id=A261C142F`.

 If you do not want to run the sample application in Docker locally, then skip to the *Entering the Azure portal* section where we will show you how to do the same in Azure without installing anything locally.

In this section, we will show you how to run the Azure Voting application on your local machine. This requires the following:

- Follow the instructions and install Git (`https://git-scm.com/downloads`) on your local machine.
- Install Docker (`https://www.docker.com/get-started`); follow the instructions in the get-started document to install the Docker engine.
- We will use the **Azure Voting** application (`https://github.com/Azure-Samples/azure-voting-app-redis`) as provided by Microsoft on GitHub.

Now let's check out what version of Docker is running on your machine by using the following command. Open your favorite command-line prompt and check the versions of the Docker components that are installed. The response will be the versions you are running locally.

```
$ docker --version
Docker version 18.06.1-ce, build e68fc7a
$docker-compose --version
docker-compose version 1.22.0, build f46880f
$docker-machine --version
docker-machine version 0.15.0, build b48dc28d
```

It is time to get the application code from GitHub and run the Azure Voting application locally. You will see how easy it is to do that. In your command-line window, type the following commands:

```
$ git clone https://github.com/Azure-Samples/azure-voting-app-redis.git
```

Change the directory to see the content of the cloned repository:

```
$ cd azure-voting-app-redis
```

Now let's take a sneak peek at the `docker-compose.yaml` file. The Azure Voting application is composed of three containers:

1. **Azure-vote-back**, the backend service of the application
2. **Azure-vote-front**, the web application frontend
3. **Redis DB**, the default Redis image

The YAML files describe the services, the container images, and ports that compose the application. You can also see that the application is using a default Redis Docker image. If you open the YAML file, it will look like this:

```
version: '3'
services:
 azure-vote-back:
 image: redis
 container_name: azure-vote-back
 ports:
 - "6379:6379"

 azure-vote-front:
 build: ./azure-vote
 image: azure-vote-front
 container_name: azure-vote-front
 environment:
 REDIS: azure-vote-back
 ports:
 - "8080:80"
```

Use the `docker-compose.yaml` file we just explored to build the container images, download the Redis image, and run the application:

```
$ docker-compose up -d
```

Let's check the containers running on the local machine:

```
$ docker ps
CONTAINER ID            IMAGE               COMMAND                 CREATED
STATUS                  PORTS                           NAMES
9062b399fd6e            azure-vote-front    "/entrypoint.sh /sta..."  20 hours
ago         Up 20 hours         443/tcp, 0.0.0.0:8080->80/tcp   azure-
vote-front
09befdf2128a            redis               "docker-entrypoint.s..."  20 hours
ago         Up 20 hours     0.0.0.0:6379->6379/tcp          azure-
vote-back
```

Last, but not least, let's start the Azure Voting app running on your local machine by going to your web browser and typing `http://localhost:8080`. The application will be loaded, and you can vote for cats or dogs. Happy voting!

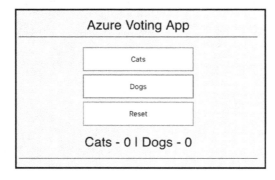

Before moving on to the Azure portal, clean up the Docker images and resources with the following:

```
$ docker-compose down
Stopping azure-vote-front ... done
Stopping azure-vote-back  ... done
Removing azure-vote-front ... done
Removing azure-vote-back  ... done
Removing network azure-voting-app-redis_default
```

In the next sections, you will use Azure portal to deploy and run the same application on AKS in Microsoft Azure.

 Provide the GitHub URL for the code in the chapter (setup instructions should be on the GitHub page). Create a GitHub folder named chX, where X is the chapter number, for example, ch1.

Entering the Azure portal

Till we get to an all command-line method of operation (aka the DevOps way), we will be utilizing Azure Portal for most of our use cases. Even when we are using command-line functions for most of our operations, Azure Portal is where you can quickly check the status of your infrastructure. Familiarity with Azure Portal is essential for running your AKS.

Creating an Azure portal account

 If you already have an account with Azure and/or are familiar with Azure Portal, you can skip this section.

Here we will show you how to get started with a free account.

 In order to keep your trial account separate, you probably want to start the browser in Incognito or Private Browsing mode.

1. Go to `https://azure.microsoft.com/en-us/free/`

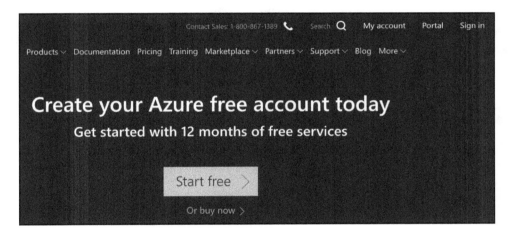

2. Click the **Start free >** button.

3. Create a new account:

4. Unless you want to use your existing email address, select **Get a new email address**:

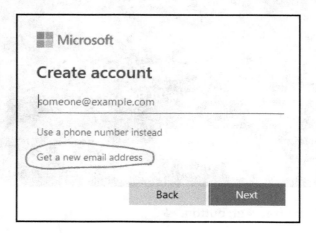

5. Give an email address name that you will remember:

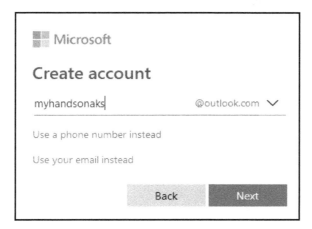

    Do not forget this email address. You will have to use this email address to log on to Azure Portal throughout the book.

6. Create your password:

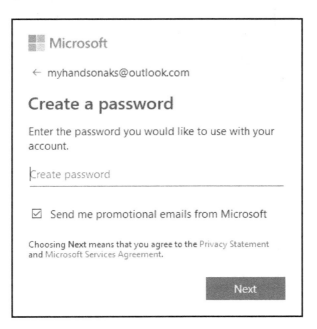

As before, do not forget your password! We don't want to know it. We are definitely not responsible for it! (If you want fund our complete Lego Star Wars collectible sets, then do let us know.)

7. Pass your **are you human** test:

8. Select **Stay signed in?** to reduce some finger wear and tear (unless you are paranoid. If you are, then are you sure you want to use Microsoft services?):

9. To get started on Azure, you will need a credit card or a phone to back you up. You will not be charged till you cross your $200 limit (at least, that's what Azure says. Use at your own risk):

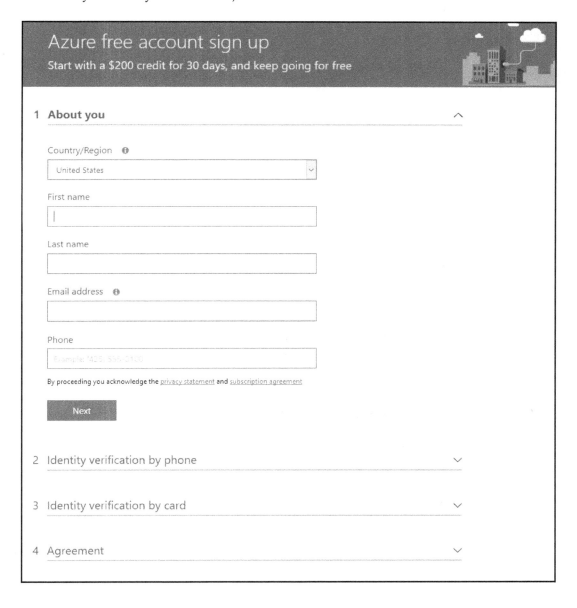

10. You still need your credit card to sign up:

 The free account is valid *only* for 30 days. Please finish the book by then and delete your account if you do not want to be charged after the trial. (Remember getting new emails is free.)

Congratulations! Finally, you should have access to the `https://portal.azure.com` portal. Take the 30-second **Start Tour**. In the book examples that follow, we are going to assume that you have created a new account.

Navigating the Azure portal

We are going to jump straight in by creating our **Azure Kubernetes Service** (**AKS**). By doing so, we are also going to familiarize ourselves with the Azure portal. Please note that we are going to ask you to blindly click here and there. We will explain the different concepts later in the appropriate context or as side notes. For now, trust us, we are engineers (at least we used to be).

Creating your first AKS

On the top center where the search icon is, type this:

`aks`

You will see **Kubernetes services** under **SERVICES**. Click on it:

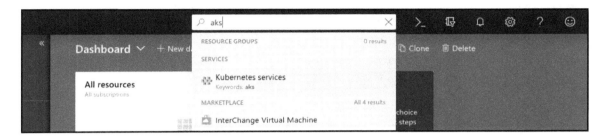

You have to add a new **Resource Group**. Type handsonaks and myfirstakscluster for the cluster name:

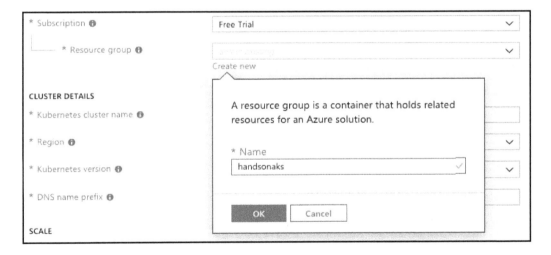

 Use the previous names for **Resource Group** and **Cluster Name**. We will be using those repeatedly in the future. If you type anything else, you need to substitute the right group and name it appropriately.

The following settings were tested by us to work reliably with the free account.

Since it is just our sample application and to extend your free credits as much as possible, we will choose only one node with one vCPU. Click on **Change size**:

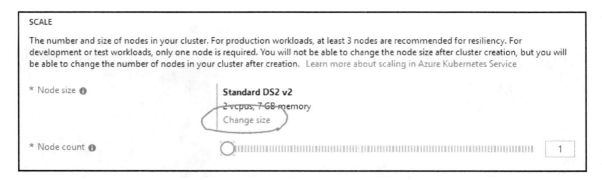

 Your free account has a four-core limit that will be violated if we go with the defaults.

Select **DS1_v2** as follows:

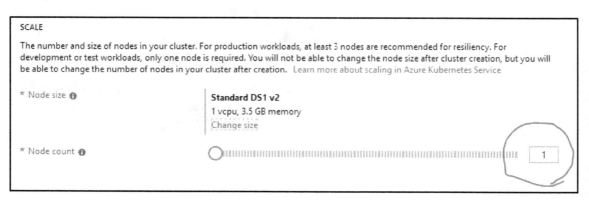

Change the **vCPU** to 1:

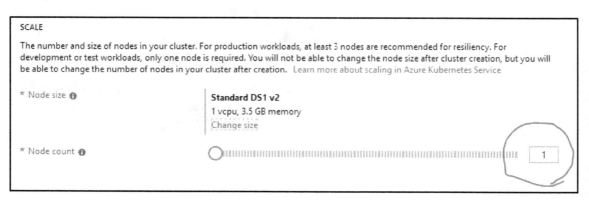

Like all good things in life, if they worked out of the box, we would be out of a job. There is one more thing we have to set, apart from the changes we needed to make it work under the free trial. Choose **West US 2** for **Region** before clicking on **Review + Create**:

Click on **Create**:

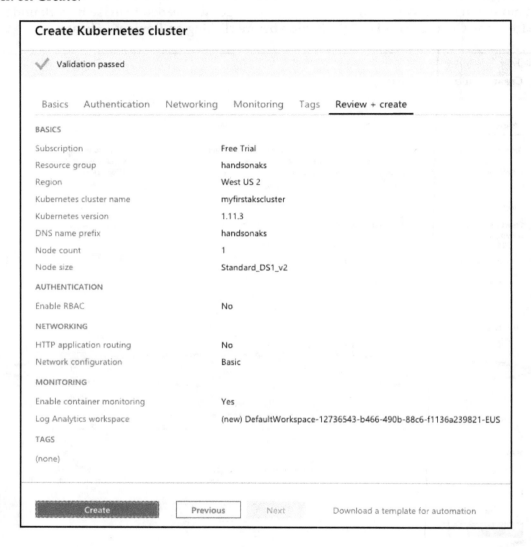

Create Kubernetes cluster

✓ Validation passed

Basics   Authentication   Networking   Monitoring   Tags   **Review + create**

BASICS

Subscription	Free Trial
Resource group	handsonaks
Region	West US 2
Kubernetes cluster name	myfirstakscluster
Kubernetes version	1.11.3
DNS name prefix	handsonaks
Node count	1
Node size	Standard_DS1_v2

AUTHENTICATION

Enable RBAC	No

NETWORKING

HTTP application routing	No
Network configuration	Basic

MONITORING

Enable container monitoring	Yes
Log Analytics workspace	(new) DefaultWorkspace-12736543-b466-490b-88c6-f1136a239821-EUS

TAGS

(none)

Create   Previous   Next   Download a template for automation

You have worked really hard. You deserve a coffee break. Well, maybe not. In any case, as of now, it takes at least 10-20 minutes to create a cluster on AKS. So, you might as well.

If you have been really good this year, you should see this:

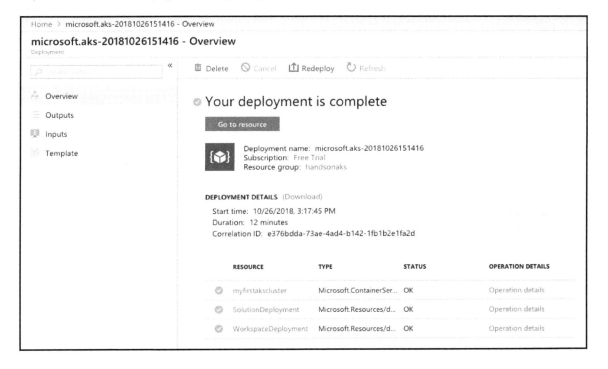

If you were not, we are not judging you; we can always blame Microsoft. For example, this is the error we got for the quota limitation as shown in the following screenshot. Double-check the settings (you thought you were smarter than us, didn't you? We know you ... we did the same when following the documentation) and try again:

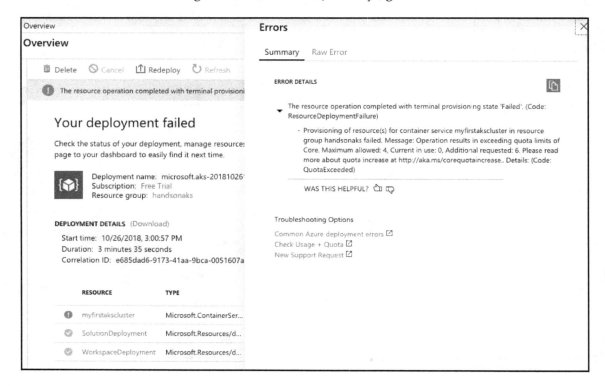

Using Azure Cloud Shell

Once you have a successful deployment, it is time to play. As promised, we will do it all from the Azure portal with no client installs.

The toughest part of this assignment is finding the small icon near the search bar:

Go ahead. Click on it.

First the portal will ask you to select either PowerShell or Bash as your default shell experience.

Next, the portal will ask you to create a storage account; just confirm and create it.

You might still get this:

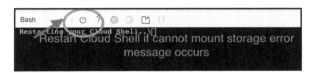

Restart Cloud Shell if cannot mount storage error message occurs

Click on the power button; it should restart, and you should see something similar to this:

You can pull the splitter/divider up to see more of the shell:

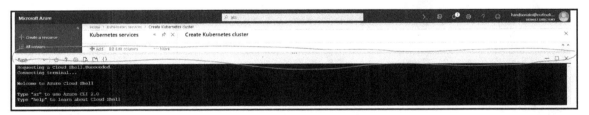

On the shell, we need to first install `kubectl`. This is the command-line tool used for many operations when operating and maintaining Kubernetes clusters. Furthermore, `kubectl` is already installed for you on Azure Cloud Shell.

You need the credentials to access your cluster. For example, on the shell, type the following command:

```
az aks get-credentials --resource-group handsonaks --name myfirstakscluster
```

The preceding command will set the correct values in ~/.kube/config so that kubectl can access it.

To verify that you have access, type the following:

```
kubectl get all
```

You should see something like this:

```
NAME                                           READY   STATUS    RESTARTS   AGE
pod/heapster-7b74498c4b-9qhtp                  2/2     Running   0          9d
pod/kube-dns-v20-668899dbdc-knjqx              3/3     Running   0          9d
pod/kube-dns-v20-668899dbdc-mwqnv              3/3     Running   0          9d
pod/kube-proxy-11156                           1/1     Running   0          9d
pod/kube-svc-redirect-r7dzp                    2/2     Running   0          9d
pod/kubernetes-dashboard-55c64b9ddb-4rhx9      1/1     Running   0          9d
pod/metrics-server-76f76c6bfd-ns979            1/1     Running   0          9d
pod/omsagent-h869k                             1/1     Running   1          9d
pod/omsagent-rs-5f6cdd5476-dptcw               1/1     Running   0          9d
pod/tunnelfront-565799fcb8-kjc9d               1/1     Running   0          9d

NAME                           TYPE        CLUSTER-IP     EXTERNAL-IP   PORT(S)         AGE
service/heapster               ClusterIP   10.0.234.139   <none>        80/TCP          9d
service/kube-dns               ClusterIP   10.0.0.10      <none>        53/UDP,53/TCP   9d
service/kubernetes-dashboard   ClusterIP   10.0.42.38     <none>        80/TCP          9d
service/metrics-server         ClusterIP   10.0.186.26    <none>        443/TCP         9d

NAME                                  DESIRED   CURRENT   READY   UP-TO-DATE   AVAILABLE   NODE SELECTOR                  AGE
daemonset.apps/kube-proxy             1         1         1       1            1           beta.kubernetes.io/os=linux    9d
daemonset.apps/kube-svc-redirect      1         1         1       1            1           beta.kubernetes.io/os=linux    9d
daemonset.apps/omsagent               1         1         1       1            1           beta.kubernetes.io/os=linux    9d

NAME                                  DESIRED   CURRENT   UP-TO-DATE   AVAILABLE   AGE
deployment.apps/heapster              1         1         1            1           9d
deployment.apps/kube-dns-v20          2         2         2            2           9d
deployment.apps/kubernetes-dashboard  1         1         1            1           9d
deployment.apps/metrics-server        1         1         1            1           9d
deployment.apps/omsagent-rs           1         1         1            1           9d
deployment.apps/tunnelfront           1         1         1            1           9d

NAME                                             DESIRED   CURRENT   READY   AGE
replicaset.apps/heapster-5f8d5688                0         0         0       9d
replicaset.apps/heapster-7b74498c4b              1         1         1       9d
replicaset.apps/kube-dns-v20-668899dbdc          2         2         2       9d
replicaset.apps/kubernetes-dashboard-55c64b9ddb  1         1         1       9d
replicaset.apps/metrics-server-76f76c6bfd        1         1         1       9d
replicaset.apps/omsagent-rs-5f6cdd5476           1         1         1       9d
replicaset.apps/tunnelfront-565799fcb8           1         1         1       9d
```

There is no need to worry whether all of these are exactly matching or what each item is. For now, our goal is to to be comfortable with `kubectl` and to ensure that the connection works.

If you are seeing **connection refused** or other access-related errors, double-check the entries in the following command:
`az aks get-credentials --resource-group` **handsonaks** `--name` **myfirstakscluster**

You are all connected now. We are going to launch our first application now.

We are going to use the `vi` command-line editor. It is generally confusing to use at first, but you can use the online code editor shown in the next section.

For the online code editor, type the following:

```
PS Azure:\&gt; code .
```

For `vi`, type this:

```
vi azure-vote.yaml
```

If you are in `vi`, type `i` to get into the insert mode.

On a different browser, open `https://docs.microsoft.com/en-us/azure/aks/kubernetes-walkthrough`. We will use the code directly there for now.

Go to the section that has the code for `azure-vote.yaml` and click on the **Copy** button:

Create a file named `azure-vote.yaml` and copy into it the following YAML code. If you are working in Azure Cloud Shell, this file can be created using vi or Nano as if working on a virtual or physical system.

yaml   📋 Copy

```yaml
apiVersion: apps/v1
kind: Deployment
metadata:
  name: azure-vote-back
spec:
  replicas: 1
  selector:
    matchLabels:
      app: azure-vote-back
  template:
    metadata:
      labels:
        app: azure-vote-back
    spec:
      containers:
      - name: azure-vote-back
        image: redis
        resources:
          requests:
            cpu: 100m
            memory: 128Mi
          limits:
            cpu: 250m
            memory: 256Mi
        ports:
        - containerPort: 6379
          name: redis
---
```

We have included the code from the Azure website for your convenience:

```yaml
apiVersion: apps/v1
kind: Deployment
metadata:
  name: azure-vote-back
spec:
  replicas: 1
  selector:
    matchLabels:
      app: azure-vote-back
  template:
    metadata:
      labels:
        app: azure-vote-back
    spec:
      containers:
        - name: azure-vote-back
```

```
        image: redis
        resources:
          requests:
            cpu: 100m
            memory: 128Mi
          limits:
            cpu: 250m
            memory: 256Mi
        ports:
        - containerPort: 6379
          name: redis
---
apiVersion: v1
kind: Service
metadata:
  name: azure-vote-back
spec:
  ports:
  - port: 6379
  selector:
    app: azure-vote-back
---
apiVersion: apps/v1
kind: Deployment
metadata:
  name: azure-vote-front
spec:
  replicas: 1
  selector:
    matchLabels:
      app: azure-vote-front
  template:
    metadata:
      labels:
        app: azure-vote-front
    spec:
      containers:
      - name: azure-vote-front
        image: microsoft/azure-vote-front:v1
        resources:
          requests:
            cpu: 100m
            memory: 128Mi
          limits:
            cpu: 250m
            memory: 256Mi
        ports:
        - containerPort: 80
```

```
        env:
        - name: REDIS
          value: "azure-vote-back"
    ---
    apiVersion: v1
    kind: Service
    metadata:
      name: azure-vote-front
    spec:
      type: LoadBalancer
      ports:
      - port: 80
      selector:
        app: azure-vote-front
```

Back on the Azure online code editor, paste the content of the file.

Then, click on the ... in the right-hand corner to save the file as `azure-vote.yaml`:

The file should be saved. You can check by typing the following:

```
cat azure-vote.yaml
```

Hitting the *Tab* button expands the file name in Linux. In the preceding scenario, if you hit *Tab* after typing `az` it should expand to `azure-vote.yaml`.

Now, let's launch the application:

```
kubectl create -f azure-vote.yaml
```

Now we wait.

You can check the progress by typing the following:

```
kubectl get pods
```

Typing `kubectl` can become tedious. We generally use the `alias` command to make our life easier. We use `alias kc=kubectl`. After running the preceding command, we can just use `kc get pods`.

Hit the *Up* arrow and press *return* till you get the status as all pods running. It does take some time to set up everything, which you can check by typing the following:

```
kubectl get all --all-namespaces
```

The following screenshot illustrates the output of the preceding command:

```
ab443838-9b3e-4811-b287-74e417a9@Azure:~$ kc get all --all-namespaces
NAMESPACE     NAME                                          READY   STATUS             RESTARTS   AGE
default       pod/azure-vote-back-5db676f7d-d7hn2           1/1     Running            0          2m
default       pod/azure-vote-front-559f8954f4-89v8x         0/1     ContainerCreating  0          2m
kube-system   pod/heapster-7b74498c4b-9qhtp                 2/2     Running            0          1d
kube-system   pod/kube-dns-v20-668899dbdc-knjqx             3/3     Running            0          1d
kube-system   pod/kube-dns-v20-668899dbdc-mwqnv             3/3     Running            0          1d
kube-system   pod/kube-proxy-11156                          1/1     Running            0          1d
kube-system   pod/kube-svc-redirect-r7dzp                   2/2     Running            0          1d
kube-system   pod/kubernetes-dashboard-55c64b9ddb-4rhx9     1/1     Running            0          1d
kube-system   pod/metrics-server-76f76c6bfd-ns979           1/1     Running            0          1d
kube-system   pod/omsagent-h869k                            1/1     Running            1          1d
kube-system   pod/omsagent-rs-5f6cdd5476-dptcw              1/1     Running            0          1d
kube-system   pod/tunnelfront-565799fcb8-kjc9d              1/1     Running            0          1d
```

It is most likely that it will be stuck on the previous step. If you are impatient, you can also type to see whether the frontend image has been pulled:

```
kubectl get events | grep -i pulled
```

The following screenshot illustrates the output of the preceding command:

Once you see **Pulled** for the frontend, type the following to ensure that everything is running:

```
ab443838-9b3e-4811-b287-74e417a9@Azure:~$ kc get all
NAME                                      READY   STATUS
pod/azure-vote-back-5db676f7d-d7hn2       1/1     Running
pod/azure-vote-front-559f8954f4-89v8x     1/1     Running
```

In order to access it publicly, we need to wait for one more thing. We could type commands repeatedly *or* let Kubernetes know once a service is up and running. Now we want to know the public IP of the load balancer so that we can access it.

Type the following command:

```
kubectl get service azure-vote-front --watch
```

Wait for the public IP to appear and then press *Ctrl + C* to exit the watch:

```
b443838-9b3e-4811-b287-74e417a9@Azure:~$ kubectl get service azure-vote-front --watch
AME                TYPE           CLUSTER-IP    EXTERNAL-IP     PORT(S)        AGE
zure-vote-front    LoadBalancer   10.0.211.0    13.77.147.247   80:30413/TCP   9m
Cab443838-9b3e-4811-b287-74e417a9@Azure:~$
```

Note the external IP address, and type it on a browser. You should see this:

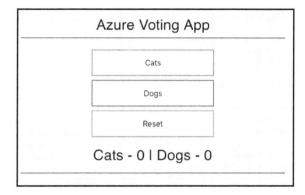

Click on **Cats** or **Dogs** (I would go with **Dogs**) and watch the count go up.

You have now launched your own cluster and your first Kubernetes application. Note the effort of connecting the frontend and the backend and exposing it to the outside world along with providing storage for the services was all taken care of by Kubernetes.

Summary

By the end of this chapter, we are now able to access and navigate the Azure portal to perform all the functions required to launch AKS and also to use the free trial on Azure to your advantage while learning the ins and outs of AKS and other Azure services. We launched our own AKS cluster with the ability to customize configurations if required using Azure Portal. We also learned to use Azure Cloud Shell without installing anything on your computer. This is important for all the upcoming sections, where you will be doing a lot more than launching simple applications. Finally, we launched a publicly accessible service that works! The skeleton of this application is the same for the complex applications that you will be launching in the next sections.

Section 2: Deploying on AKS

Section 2 focuses on getting an application running on AKS. Readers will be able to deploy, scale, and monitor an application on AKS. Readers will also learn how to use Kubernetes' RBAC on AKS through integration with Azure AD.

The following chapters will be covered in this section:

Application Deployment on AKS

3

In this chapter, we will look at the details of deploying an application on the **Azure Kubernetes Service** (**AKS**). An application consists of multiple parts, and we will build an application one step at a time, while explaining the conceptual model behind it. You will be able to easily adapt the steps in this chapter to deploy any other application on AKS. The sample guestbook application will be deployed on AKS. The reader will understand the usefulness of various Kubernetes concepts, such as Pods, **Replication Controllers** (**RCs**), services, ConfigMaps, Namespaces, and Deployments. We will introduce deployment helpers, such as Helm, to streamline the deployment process.

The following topics will be covered in this chapter:

- Deploying the sample guestbook application
- Full deployment of the sample guestbook application
- The helm way of installing complex applications

Technical requirements

You'll need a modern browser, such as Chrome, Firefox, Safari, or Edge.

Deploying the sample guestbook application

In this chapter, we will deploy the classic guestbook sample Kubernetes application. We will be mostly following the steps from `https://Kubernetes.io/docs/tutorials/stateless-application/guestbook/` with some modifications. We employ these modifications to do the following:

- Make the solution more AKS friendly
- Show additional concepts, such as ConfigMaps, that are not present in the original sample

As mentioned in the Kubernetes documentation, you will be deploying a simple, multi-tier web application. You know it is a good sign for a platform when the documentation says it is a simple application that has master/slave backends and a scalable fronted. The guest book solution is also categorized as a stateless application because the frontend doesn't store any state. It is stateful for the single instance of Redis master, which stores all the guestbook entries.

You will be using this application as the basis for testing out the scaling of the backend and the frontend independently in the next chapter.

Introducing the application

The application stores and displays guestbook entries. You can use it to record the opinions of all the people who visit your model railroad display, for example. Along the way, we will explain Kubernetes concepts such as Deployments and replication controllers.

The application uses PHP with Redis backends for this purpose.

Deploying the first master

You are going to deploy the Redis master, which you will delete in the next step. This is done for no other reason than for you to learn about ConfigMaps.

Let's do this.

1. Open your friendly cloud shell, as highlighted in the following screenshot:

2. Type the following:

```
kubectl apply -f
https://k8s.io/examples/application/guestbook/redis-master-deployment.yaml
```

It will take some time for it to download and start running. While you wait, let me explain the command you just typed and executed. Let's start by exploring the content of the yaml file you used:

```
 1 apiVersion: apps/v1 # for versions before 1.9.0 use apps/v1beta2
 2 kind: Deployment
 3 metadata:
 4   name: redis-master
 5   labels:
 6     app: redis
 7 spec:
 8   selector:
 9     matchLabels:
10       app: redis
11       role: master
12       tier: backend
13   replicas: 1
14   template:
15     metadata:
16       labels:
17         app: redis
18         role: master
19         tier: backend
20     spec:
21       containers:
22       - name: master
23         image: k8s.gcr.io/redis:e2e # or just image: redis
24         resources:
25           requests:
26             cpu: 100m
27             memory: 100Mi
28         ports:
29         - containerPort: 6379
```

We will go inside the code to get straight to the meat of it:

- **Line 23**: Says what Docker image we are going to run. In this case, it is the redis image tagged with e2e (presumably the latest image of redis that successfully passed its end-to-end [e2e] tests).
- **Lines 28-29**: Say this container is going to listen on port 6379.
- **Line 22**: Gives this container a name, which is master.

- **Lines 24-27**: Sets the `cpu/memory` resources requested for the container. In this case, the request is 0.1 CPU, which is equal to `100m` and is also often referred to as 100 millicores. The memory requested is `100Mi`, or `104857600` bytes, which is equal to `~105M` (`https://Kubernetes .io/docs/concepts/configuration/ manage-compute-resources-container/`). You can also set `cpu` and `memory` limits the same way.

This is very similar to the arguments you will give to Docker to run a particular container image. If you had to run this manually, you would start and end getting something like the following:

```
docker run -d k8s.gcr.io/redis:e2e # run the redis docker image with tag
e2e in detached mode

docker run --name named_master -d k8s.gcr.io/redis:e2e # run the image with
the name test_master

docker run --name net_master -p 6379:6379 -d k8s.gcr.io/redis:e2e # expose
the port 6379

docker run --name master -p 6379:6379 -m 100M -c 100m -d
k8s.gcr.io/redis:e2e # set the cpu and memory limits
```

The container spec (lines 21-29) tells Kubernetes to run the specified container with the supplied arguments. So far, Kubernetes has not provided us anything more than what we could have typed in as a Docker command. Let's continue with the explanation of the code:

- **Line 13**: It tells Kubernetes that we need exactly only one copy of the Redis master running. This is a key aspect of the declarative nature of Kubernetes. You provide a description of the containers your applications need to run (in this case, only one replica of the Redis master) and Kubernetes takes care of it.
- **Lines 14-19**: Adds labels to the running instance so that it can be grouped and connected to other containers. We will discuss them later to see how they are used.
- **Line 2**: Tells we would like a **Deployment** to be performed. When Kubernetes started, Replication Controllers were used (and are still used widely) to launch containers. You can still do most of the work you need using just Replication Controllers. **Deployment** adds convenience to managing RC. Deployments provide mechanisms to perform rollout changes and rollback if required. You can specify the strategy you would like to use when pushing an update (Rolling Update or Recreate).

- **Line 4-6**: Gives the Deployment a name, which is `redis-master`.
- **Line 7-12**: Let's us specify the containers that this Deployment will manage. In our example, it says that this Deployment will select and manage all containers for which labels match (`app == redis`, `role == master`, `tier == backend`). The preceding exactly matches the labels in lines 14-19.

Examining the deployment

The `redis-master` deployment should be complete by now. On Azure Cloud Shell, type the following:

```
kubectl get all
```

You should get an output that looks something like this:

```
NAME READY STATUS RESTARTS AGE
pod/redis-master-6b464554c8-554p8 1/1 Running 0 3h

NAME TYPE CLUSTER-IP EXTERNAL-IP PORT(S) AGE
service/Kubernetes  ClusterIP 10.0.0.1 <none> 443/TCP 4h

NAME DESIRED CURRENT UP-TO-DATE AVAILABLE AGE
deployment.apps/redis-master 1 1 1 1 3h

NAME DESIRED CURRENT READY AGE
replicaset.apps/redis-master-6b464554c8 1 1 1 3h
```

You can see that we have a deployment named `redis-master`. It controls a replica set of `redis-master-<random id>`. Digging deeper, you will also find that the Replica Set is controlling **Pod** (a group of Docker containers that should be run together): `redis-master-<replica set random id&gt;->random id&gt;`.

More details can be obtained by typing `kubectl describe <instance -name>`, as follows:

```
kubectl describe deployment/redis-master
```

This will give us the following output:

```
Name: redis-master
 Namespace: default
 CreationTimestamp: Wed, 26 Dec 2018 01:47:56 +0000
 Labels: app=redis
 Annotations: deployment.Kubernetes .io/revision=1
 kubectl.Kubernetes .io/last-applied-
```

```
configuration={"apiVersion":"apps/v1","kind":"Deployment","metadata":{"anno
tations":{},"labels":{"app":"redis"},"name":"redis-
master","namespace":"default"},"spec":{...
 Selector: app=redis,role=master,tier=backend
 Replicas: 1 desired | 1 updated | 1 total | 1 available | 0 unavailable
 StrategyType: RollingUpdate
 MinReadySeconds: 0
 RollingUpdateStrategy: 25% max unavailable, 25% max surge
 Pod Template:
 Labels: app=redis
 role=master
 tier=backend
 Containers:
 master:
 Image: k8s.gcr.io/redis:e2e
 Port: 6379/TCP
 Host Port: 0/TCP
 Requests:
 cpu: 100m
 memory: 100Mi
 Environment: <none>
 Mounts: <none>
 Volumes: <none>
 Conditions:
 Type Status Reason
 ---- ------ ------
 Available True MinimumReplicasAvailable
 Progressing True NewReplicaSetAvailable
 OldReplicaSets: <none>
 NewReplicaSet: redis-master-6b464554c8 (1/1 replicas created)
 Events: <none>
```

In true internet fashion, launching an application without any environment-specific configuration has already become obsolete. We will introduce a new concept called **ConfigMaps** and then resume the regularly-scheduled program. First, we need to clean up, and we can do so by running the following command:

```
kubectl delete deployment/redis-master
```

You will see the following output:

```
deployment.extensions "redis-master" deleted
```

Redis master

There was nothing wrong with the previous deployment. In practical use cases, it would be rare that you would launch an application without some configuration settings. In this case, we are going to set the following configuration settings for `redis-master` (from the example in `https://Kubernetes.io/docs/tutorials/configuration/configure-redis-using-configmap/`).

Copy and paste the following two lines into the Azure Cloud Shell editor and save it as `redis-config`:

```
maxmemory 2mb
maxmemory-policy allkeys-lru
```

 The online editor is limited and surprisingly doesn't have support for creating a new file, not to worry. In this case, type `touch redis-config`. Then `code redis-config` works. Or you can open the empty file using the open file command on the online code editor.

Now we can create the ConfigMap using the following code:

```
kubectl create configmap example-redis-config --from-file=redis-config
```

You should get this as the output:

```
configmap/example-redis-config created
```

We will use the same trick to get the scoop on this ConfigMap:

```
kubectl describe configmap/example-redis-config
```

The output should look like this:

```
Name:         example-redis-config
Namespace:    default
Labels:       <none>
Annotations:  <none>

Data
====
redis-config:
----
maxmemory 2mb
maxmemory-policy allkeys-lru
Events:   <none>
```

Creating from the command line is not very portable. It would be better if we could describe the preceding code in a yaml file. If only there was a command that would get the same information in yaml format. Not to worry, kubectl has the get command:

```
kubectl get -o yaml configmap/example-redis-config
```

The preceding command gets close to what we want as shown:

```
apiVersion: v1
data:
  redis-config: |-
    maxmemory 2mb
    maxmemory-policy allkeys-lru
kind: ConfigMap
metadata:
  creationTimestamp: 2018-12-26T06:35:57Z
  name: example-redis-config
  namespace: default
  resourceVersion: "23430"
  selfLink: /api/v1/namespaces/default/configmaps/example-redis-config
  uid: 80624489-08d8-11e9-9914-82000ff4ac53
```

Let's create our yaml version of this. But first, let's delete the already-created ConfigMap:

```
kubectl delete configmap/example-redis-config
```

Copy and paste the following lines into a file named example-redis-config.yaml, and then save the file:

```
apiVersion: v1
data:
  redis-config: |-
    maxmemory 2mb
    maxmemory-policy allkeys-lru
kind: ConfigMap
metadata:
  name: example-redis-config
  namespace: default
```

Use the touch trick to open the file on the online code editor.

kubectl get -o yaml is a useful trick to get a deployable yaml file from a running system. It takes care of tricky yaml indentation and saves you from spending hours trying to get the format right.

ConfigMap is a portable way of configuring containers without having specialized images for each configuration. ConfigMap has a key-value pair for data that needs to be set on a container. In this case, `redis-config` is the key and `maxmemory 2mbmaxmemory-policy allkeys-lru` is the value.

Run the following command:

```
kubectl create -f example-redis-config
```

The output should be as follows:

```
configmap/example-redis-config created
```

Next, run the following command:

```
kubectl describe configmap/example-redis-config
```

The preceding command returns the same output as the previous one:

```
Name:           example-redis-config
Namespace:      default
Labels:         <none>
Annotations:    <none>

Data
====
redis-config:
----
maxmemory 2mb
maxmemory-policy allkeys-lru
Events:  <none>
```

Now that we have ConfigMap defined, let's use it. Modify `redis-master-deployment.yaml` to use ConfigMap, as follows:

```
apiVersion: apps/v1 # for versions before 1.9.0 use apps/v1beta2
kind: Deployment
metadata:
  name: redis-master
  labels:
    app: redis
spec:
  selector:
    matchLabels:
      app: redis
      role: master
      tier: backend
  replicas: 1
```

```
    template:
      metadata:
        labels:
          app: redis
          role: master
          tier: backend
      spec:
        containers:
        - name: master
          image: Kubernetes /redis:v1
          env:
          - name: MASTER
            value: "true"
          volumeMounts:
          - mountPath: /redis-master
            name: config
          resources:
            requests:
              cpu: 100m
              memory: 100Mi
          ports:
          - containerPort: 6379
        volumes:
          - name: config
            configMap:
              name: example-redis-config
              items:
              - key: redis-config
                path: redis.conf
```

We are using a different image `Kubernetes/redis:v1` that reads `redis-config` from `/redis-master/redis.conf` (instead of the usual `/etc/redis/redis.conf` in the other image). As usual, we are going to explain the new sections with line numbers:

```
 1 apiVersion: apps/v1 # for versions before 1.9.0 use apps/v1beta2
 2 kind: Deployment
 3 metadata:
 4   name: redis-master
 5   labels:
 6     app: redis
 7 spec:
 8   selector:
 9     matchLabels:
10       app: redis
11       role: master
12       tier: backend
13   replicas: 1
14   template:
```

```
15      metadata:
16        labels:
17          app: redis
18          role: master
19          tier: backend
20      spec:
21        containers:
22        - name: master
23          image: Kubernetes /redis:v1
24          env:
25          - name: MASTER
26            value: "true"
27          volumeMounts:
28          - mountPath: /redis-master
29            name: config
30          resources:
31            requests:
32              cpu: 100m
33              memory: 100Mi
34          ports:
35          - containerPort: 6379
36        volumes:
37        - name: config
38          configMap:
39            name: example-redis-config
40            items:
41            - key: redis-config
42              path: redis.conf
```

The following lines will give a detailed explanation of the preceding code:

- **Lines 24-26**: Show another way of configuring your running container. This method uses environment variables. In Docker form, this would be equivalent to `docker run -e "MASTER=TRUE".--name master -p 6379:6379 -m 100M -c 100m -d Kubernetes /redis:v1 #` set the environment variable `MASTER=TRUE`. Your application can read the environment variable settings for its configuration. Check out `https://12factor.net/config` to see why this is a very powerful idea.
- **Lines 27-28**: Mounts the named volume (config that is defined in lines 36-42) at the `/redis-master` path on the running container. Since this is bind mount, it will hide whatever is exists on `/redis-master` on the original container.

In Docker terms, it would be equivalent to

```
docker run -v config:/redis-master.-e "MASTER=TRUE" --name
master -p 6379:6379 -m 100M -c 100m -d Kubernetes /redis:v1
# mount the config folder at redis-master on the container.
```

- **Line 36-42**: Here is where Kubernetes takes the config as `ENV vars` to the next level.
- **Line 37**: Gives the volume the `config`.
- **Line 38-39**: Declares this volume should be loaded from the ConfigMap `example-redis-config` (which has to be already defined [unless declared optional]). We have defined this already, so we are good.
- **Line 40-42**: Here is where the Kubernetes magic comes in. Configure a Pod with ConfigMap (`https://kubernetes.io/docs/tasks/configure-pod-container/configure-pod-configmap/#use-configmap-defined-environment-variables-in-pod-commands`). This shows different ways you can load the config on to a pod. Here we are loading the value of the `redis-config` key (the two-line maxmemory settings) as a file called `redis.conf`.

We can check whether the settings were applied by running the following commands:

```
kc exec -it redis-master-<pod-id> redis-cli
127.0.0.1:6379&gt; CONFIG GET maxmemory
1) "maxmemory"
2) "2097152"
127.0.0.1:6379&gt; CONFIG GET maxmemory-policy
1) "maxmemory-policy"
2) "allkeys-lru"
127.0.0.1:6379&gt;exit
```

You can see how this works by running the following:

```
kc exec -it redis-master-<pod-id> bash
root@redis-master-585bd9d8fb-p9qml:/data# ps
bash: ps: command not found
root@redis-master-585bd9d8fb-p9qml:/data# cat
/proc/1/cmdline
sh-c/run.sh
root@redis-master-585bd9d8fb-p9qml:/data# cat /run.sh
|grep redis.conf
redis-server /redis-master/redis.conf
perl -pi -e "s/%master-ip%/${master}/" /redis-
slave/redis.conf
perl -pi -e "s/%master-port%/6379/" /redis-
slave/redis.conf
```

```
redis-server /redis-slave/redis.conf
root@redis-master-585bd9d8fb-p9qml:/data# cat /run.sh
|grep MASTER
if [[ "${MASTER}" == "true" ]]; then
root@redis-master-585bd9d8fb-p9qml:/data# cat /redis-
master/redis.conf
maxmemory 2mb
maxmemory-policy allkeys-lru
```

 Somehow, in this image, `ps` is not installed. Not to worry, we can get the info by examining the contents of the `cmdline` file under `pid 1`. Now we know that `run.sh` is the file that is run, so somewhere in that `redis.conf` file from ConfigMap mounted at `/redis-master` would be used. So we grep `redis.conf`. For sure, we can see `redis-server` when it is started, when MASTER=TRUE uses the config from `/redis-master/redis.conf`. To make sure that Kubernetes did its magic, we examine the contents of `redis.conf` by running `cat /redis-master/redis.conf` and, lo and behold, it is exactly the values we specified in the ConfigMap `example-redis-conf`.

To repeat, you have just performed the most important and tricky part of configuring cloud-native applications. You have also noticed that the apps have to be modified to be cloud-friendly to read config dynamically (the old image didn't support dynamic configuration easily).

Fully deploying of the sample guestbook application

After taking a detour to get our feet wet on dynamically configuring applications using ConfigMap, we will return to our regularly-scheduled program by deploying the rest of the guestbook application. You will see the concepts of Deployment, Replica Sets, and Pods repeated again for the backends and frontends. We will introduce another key concept called **Service**. You might have also noticed the power of protocols and Docker images. Even though we switched to a different image for `redis-master`, we have an expectation that the rest of the implementation should go through without any hitches.

Exposing the Redis master service

With plain Docker, the exposed port is constrained to the host it is running. There is no support for making the service available if the host goes down. Kubernetes provides **Service**, which handles exactly that problem. Using label-matching selectors, it proxies traffic to the right pods, including load balancing. In this case, the master has only one pod, so it just ensures that, independent of which node the pod runs, the traffic is directed to that pod. To create the service, run the following command:

```
kubectl apply -f
https://k8s.io/examples/application/guestbook/redis-master-service.yaml
```

The Redis master service has the following content:

```
 1 apiVersion: v1
 2 kind: Service
 3 metadata:
 4   name: redis-master
 5   labels:
 6     app: redis
 7     role: master
 8     tier: backend
 9 spec:
10   ports:
11   - port: 6379
12     targetPort: 6379
13   selector:
14     app: redis
15     role: master
16     tier: backend
~
```

Let's now see what we have done in the preceding code:

- **Lines 1-8**: Tell Kubernetes we want a proxy service that has the same labels as our redis-master server.
- **Lines 10-12**: Say that this Service should handle traffic arriving at 6379 and forwarded to 6,379 ports of the pods that are matched by the selector defined in line 13-16
- **Line 13-16**: Used to find the pods to which the incoming traffic needs to be proxied. So, any pod with labels matching (app:redis, AND role:master AND tier:backend) is expected to handle port 6379 traffic.

We can check the properties of the service by running the following:

```
kubectl get service
NAME TYPE CLUSTER-IP EXTERNAL-IP PORT(S) AGE
Kubernetes  ClusterIP 10.0.0.1 <none> 443/TCP 1d
redis-master ClusterIP 10.0.22.146 <none> 6379/TCP 7m
```

You see that a new service, named `redis-master`, has been created. It has a cluster wide IP of `10.0.22.146` (in this case, YMMV). Note that this IP will work only within the cluster (hence the ClusterIP type). For fun, you can test this out by running the following commands:

```
ab443838-9b3e-4811-b287-74e417a9@Azure:/usr/bin$ ssh -p 6379 10.0.22.146 #
just hangs
^C
ab443838-9b3e-4811-b287-74e417a9@Azure:/usr/bin$ ssh -p 80 www.google.com #
very quick rejection
ssh_exchange_identification: Connection closed by remote host
```

To verify it does work inside the cluster, we do our exec trick again:

```
ab443838-9b3e-4811-b287-74e417a9@Azure:/usr/bin$ ssh -p 6379 10.0.22.146 #
just hangs
^C
ab443838-9b3e-4811-b287-74e417a9@Azure:/usr/bin$ ssh -p 80 www.google.com #
very quick rejection
ssh_exchange_identification: Connection closed by remote host
```

Verify that the connection actually works inside the cluster:

```
ab443838-9b3e-4811-b287-74e417a9@Azure:~$ kubectl exec -it redis-master-
<pod-id> bash
root@redis-master-585bd9d8fb-p9qml:/data# apt-get install telnet
Reading package lists... Done
...
update-alternatives: using /usr/bin/telnet.netkit to provide
/usr/bin/telnet (telnet) in auto mode
root@redis-master-585bd9d8fb-p9qml:/data# telnet 10.0.22.146 6379 #
remember that Ctrl+] is needed to "escape" from the session
Trying 10.0.22.146...
Connected to 10.0.22.146.
Escape character is '^]'.
^]
telnet&gt; quit
Connection closed.
```

You can try other ports and it won't work.

Deploying the Redis slaves

Running a single backend on the cloud is not cool. So, we run multiple slaves to handle the massive read traffic of all those who would really like to know what people think of your model railroad display. We do this by running the following command:

```
kubectl apply -f
https://k8s.io/examples/application/guestbook/redis-slave-deployment.yaml
```

The output would be something like this:

```
ab443838-9b3e-4811-b287-74e417a9@Azure:~$ kubectl apply -f
https://k8s.io/examples/application/guestbook/redis-slave-deployment.yaml
deployment.apps/redis-slave created
ab443838-9b3e-4811-b287-74e417a9@Azure:~$ kubectl get all
NAME READY STATUS RESTARTS AGE
pod/redis-master-585bd9d8fb-p9qml 1/1 Running 0 21h
pod/redis-slave-b58dc4644-2hpr7 0/1 ContainerCreating 0 3s
pod/redis-slave-b58dc4644-bz9dj 0/1 ContainerCreating 0 3s

NAME TYPE CLUSTER-IP EXTERNAL-IP PORT(S) AGE
service/Kubernetes  ClusterIP 10.0.0.1 <none> 443/TCP 1d
service/redis-master ClusterIP 10.0.22.146 <none> 6379/TCP 1h

NAME DESIRED CURRENT UP-TO-DATE AVAILABLE AGE
deployment.apps/redis-master 1 1 1 1 21h
deployment.apps/redis-slave 2 2 2 0 3s

NAME DESIRED CURRENT READY AGE
replicaset.apps/redis-master-585bd9d8fb 1 1 1 21h
replicaset.apps/redis-slave-b58dc4644 2 2 0 3s
ab443838-9b3e-4811-b287-74e417a9@Azure:~$
```

Based on the preceding output, you can guess that this time we asked 2 replicas of the redis slave pods. That is confirmed true when you examine the redis-slave-deployment.yaml file:

```
 1 apiVersion: apps/v1 # for versions before 1.9.0 use apps/v1beta2
 2 kind: Deployment
 3 metadata:
 4   name: redis-slave
 5   labels:
 6     app: redis
 7 spec:
 8   selector:
 9     matchLabels:
10       app: redis
```

```
11          role: slave
12          tier: backend
13      replicas: 2
14      template:
15        metadata:
16          labels:
17            app: redis
18            role: slave
19            tier: backend
20        spec:
21          containers:
22          - name: slave
23            image: gcr.io/google_samples/gb-redisslave:v1
24            resources:
25              requests:
26                cpu: 100m
27                memory: 100Mi
28            env:
29            - name: GET_HOSTS_FROM
30              value: dns
31              # Using `GET_HOSTS_FROM=dns` requires your cluster to
32              # provide a dns service. As of Kubernetes 1.3, DNS is a
built-in
33              # service launched automatically. However, if the cluster you
are using
34              # does not have a built-in DNS service, you can instead
35              # access an environment variable to find the master
36              # service's host. To do so, comment out the 'value: dns' line
above, and
37              # uncomment the line below:
38              # value: env
39            ports:
40            - containerPort: 6379
```

Everything is more or less the same other than the following:

- The role is declared to be a slave.
- Replicas is equal to 2.
- We are using the gb-redisslave image.
- Setting the GET_HOSTS_FROM=dns;, we can presume that the slave is going to get the master IP using DNS. Let's check whether our assumption is correct by running the following code:

```
ab443838-9b3e-4811-b287-74e417a9@Azure:~$ kubectl exec -it redis-slave-
<pod-id> bash
 root@redis-slave-b58dc4644-2hpr7:/data# cat /proc/1/cmdline
 /bin/sh-c/run.shroot@redis-slave-b58dc4644-2hpr7:/data# cat /run.sh
```

```
#!/bin/bash
#...
if [[ ${GET_HOSTS_FROM:-dns} == "env" ]]; then
redis-server --slaveof ${REDIS_MASTER_SERVICE_HOST} 6379
else
redis-server --slaveof redis-master 6379
fi
root@redis-slave-b58dc4644-2hpr7:/data# root@redis-slave-
b58dc4644-2hpr7:/data# ping redis-master
 PING redis-master.default.svc.cluster.local (10.0.22.146): 48 data bytes
```

As expected, run.sh in the image checks whether the GET_HOSTS_FROM variable is set to env. In this case, it is set to dns, so it returns false. redis-server is launched in slave mode pointing to the redis-master host as the master. If you ping redis-master, you can see it is set to the ClusterIP of the redis-master service.

Similar to the master service, we need to expose the slave service by running the following:

```
kubectl apply -f
https://k8s.io/examples/application/guestbook/redis-slave-service.yaml

apiVersion: v1
kind: Service
metadata:
  name: redis-slave
  labels:
    app: redis
    role: slave
    tier: backend
spec:
  ports:
  - port: 6379
  selector:
    app: redis
    role: slave
    tier: backend
```

The only difference between this Service and the redis-master Service is that this service proxies traffic to pods that have the role:slave label in them.

Create the redis slave service by running the following command:

```
ab443838-9b3e-4811-b287-74e417a9@Azure:~$ kubectl apply -f
https://k8s.io/examples/application/guestbook/redis-slave-service.yaml
 service/redis-slave created
ab443838-9b3e-4811-b287-74e417a9@Azure:~$ kubectl get service
NAME TYPE CLUSTER-IP EXTERNAL-IP PORT(S) AGE
```

```
Kubernetes  ClusterIP 10.0.0.1 <none> 443/TCP 1d
redis-master ClusterIP 10.0.22.146 <none>; 6379/TCP 2h
redis-slave ClusterIP 10.0.14.218 <none> 6379/TCP 3s
ab443838-9b3e-4811-b287-74e417a9@Azure:~$
```

To check whether the slave service responds at the mentioned ClusterIP and port `6379`, run the following commands:

```
kubectl run checkredisslave -it --image ubuntu
# on the terminal or run
kubectl attach <pod-name> # to get to the terminal
# apt update
apt install -y netcat # re-run apt update in case you copied the # by
mistake in the previous command
nc -vz <redis-slave ClusterIP> 6379
# you should get ... (?) open
```

Deploying and exposing the frontend

Now it's getting pretty predictable and boring (exactly how deployments should be).

Run the following command:

```
kubectl apply -f https://k8s.io/examples/application/guestbook/frontend-
deployment.yaml
```

To verify the deployment, run this code:

```
ab443838-9b3e-4811-b287-74e417a9@Azure:~$ kubectl apply -f
https://k8s.io/examples/application/guestbook/frontend-deployment.yaml
deployment.apps/frontend created
ab443838-9b3e-4811-b287-74e417a9@Azure:~$ kc get pods
NAME READY STATUS RESTARTS AGE
frontend-56f7975f44-h9d78 0/1 Pending 0 2s
frontend-56f7975f44-kw428 0/1 Pending 0 3s
frontend-56f7975f44-nt55q 0/1 Pending 0 2s
```

You don't get any points for guessing that this Deployment specifies a replica count of 3 (OK, maybe a pat in the back; we are generous people). The Deployment has the usual suspects with minor changes as shown in the following code:

```
apiVersion: apps/v1 # for versions before 1.9.0 use apps/v1beta2
kind: Deployment
metadata:
  name: frontend
  labels:
```

```
          app: guestbook
spec:
  selector:
    matchLabels:
      app: guestbook
      tier: frontend
  replicas: 3
  template:
    metadata:
      labels:
        app: guestbook
        tier: frontend
    spec:
      containers:
      - name: php-redis
        image: gcr.io/google-samples/gb-frontend:v4
        resources:
          requests:
            cpu: 100m
            memory: 100Mi
        env:
        - name: GET_HOSTS_FROM
          value: dns
          # Using `GET_HOSTS_FROM=dns` requires your cluster to
          # provide a dns service. As of Kubernetes 1.3, DNS is a built-in
          # service launched automatically. However, if the cluster you are
using
          # does not have a built-in DNS service, you can instead
          # access an environment variable to find the master
          # service's host. To do so, comment out the 'value: dns' line
above, and
          # uncomment the line below:
          # value: env
        ports:
        - containerPort: 80
```

The replica count is set to 3, the labels are set to {app:guestbook, tier:frontend}, and the image used is gb-frontend:v4.

Exposing the frontend service

In order to make it publicly available, we have to edit the service yaml file. Run the following command to download the file:

```
curl -O -L
https://k8s.io/examples/application/guestbook/frontend-service.yaml
```

Use the online editor to edit it:

```
code frontend-service.yaml
```

Comment out the NodePort line and uncomment the `type:LoadBalancer` line:

```
apiVersion: v1
kind: Service
metadata:
  name: frontend
  labels:
    app: guestbook
    tier: frontend
spec:
  # comment or delete the following line if you want to use a LoadBalancer
  # type: NodePort # line commented out
  # if your cluster supports it, uncomment the following to automatically create
  # an external load-balanced IP for the frontend service.
  type: LoadBalancer # line uncommented
  ports:
  - port: 80
  selector:
    app: guestbook
    tier: frontend
```

Next, run the following command:

```
kubectl create -f frontend-service.yaml
```

This step takes some time the first time you run it. In the background, Azure has to perform lots of magic, to make it seamless. It has to create an **Azure Load Balancer** (**ALB**), and set the port-forwarding rules to forward traffic on port 80 to internal ports of the cluster.

Run the following until there is a value in the EXTERNAL-IP column:

```
ab443838-9b3e-4811-b287-74e417a9@Azure:~$ kubectl get svc
NAME TYPE CLUSTER-IP EXTERNAL-IP PORT(S) AGE
frontend LoadBalancer 10.0.89.120 52.183.18.103 80:31761/TCP 42m
```

In the Azure portal, if you click on **All Resources** and filter on Load Balancer, you will see a **Kubernetes** Azure Load Balancer. Clicking on it shows you something similar to the following screenshot. The highlighted sections shows the connection between the public IP (that is, External-IP):80 to the internal NodePort of `31761` across all the nodes in the cluster:

The guestbook application in action

Type the public IP on your favorite browser. You should get the following screenshot:

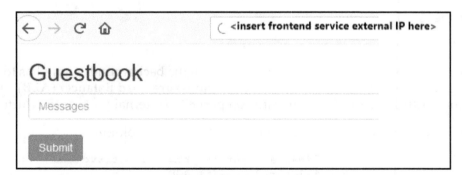

Go ahead, record your messages. It will be saved. Go crazy, open another browser and type the same IP; you will see all the messages you typed.

Congratulations, you have completed your first fully-deployed, multi-tier, cloud-native Kubernetes application!

The frontend did not show up on our first try. It turned out for the small machines we were using. Kubernetes was not able to schedule three replicas of the frontend. We had to download the `frontend-deployment.yaml` file and change the replicas to 1 and also reduce the CPU task. The problem was discovered by typing
`kubectl get events`

Alas, the preceding method of deploying has become obsolete already. We needed to give it a try for these reasons:

- For prototyping, you probably will start from one of those `yaml` files.
- The basic concepts of Deployment, Replica Sets, Services, and Pods do not change and need to be understood in detail.
- The obsolete part is not true at all.

Still, to conserve resources on our free trial virtual machines, it is better to delete the deployments we made to run the next round of the deployment by using the following commands:

```
kubectl delete deployment -l app=redis
kubectl delete service -l app=redis
kubectl delete deployment -l app=guestbook
kubectl delete service -l app=guestbook
```

The helm way of installing complex applications

As you went along the previous sections, you might have thought, This is pretty repetitive and boring. I wonder if there is a way to package everything and run it in one shot. That is a valid question, and a need when deploying complex applications in production. Helm charts is becoming the `de-facto` standard for packaging applications.

We are going to up the game by installing a complex WordPress site complete with persistence storage. We are going to do so with just one command (not counting the `helm init` command).

The helm init command

On your cloud shell, type the following:

```
helm init
```

After a couple of minutes, helm should be ready.

Installing WordPress

Run the following command:

```
helm install stable/wordpress --name handsonaks-wp --set
smtpHost=smtp.google.com --set smtpPort=25 --set smtpPassword=abcd1234 --
set smtpUser=handsonaks@gmail.com --set smtpUsername=handsonaks --set
smtpProtocol=ssl
```

That's it; Helm goes ahead and installs everything mentioned at `https://Kubernetes.io/docs/tutorials/stateful-application/mysql-wordpress-persistent-volume/`.

The command should have been just `helm install stable/wordpress --name  handsonakswp`. The reason for the extra parameters was, at the time of writing, the command did not work without the SMTP settings. For more information visit `https://github.com/bitnami/bitnami-docker-wordpress/issues/153#issuecomment-450127531`.

How did we figure out `smtpPassword` was the issue? Hint: it involved `kubectl` logs. We will go into more detail on monitoring in the next chapter.

It takes some time for Helm to install and the site to come up. We will look into a key concept, Persistent Volume Claims, while the site is loading.

Persistent Volume Claims

A process requires compute, memory, network, and storage. In the Guestbook sample, we saw how Kubernetes helps us abstract the compute, memory, and network. The same yaml files work across all cloud providers, including a cloud-specific setup of public-facing Load Balancers. The WordPress example shows how the last and the most important piece namely storage is abstracted from the underlying cloud provider.

In this case, the WordPress helm chart depends on the Maria DB helm chart (`https://github.com/helm/charts/tree/master/stable/mariadb`) for its database install. Describing the helm format would take another book; it is easier to look at the output and see what was done. Unlike stateless applications, such as our frontends, Maria DB requires careful handling of storage. We inform of this Kubernetes by defining the Maria DB deployment as StatefulSet. StatefulSet (`https://kubernetes.io/docs/concepts/workloads/controllers/statefulset/`) is like Deployment with the additional capability of ordering, and uniqueness of the pods. The previous statement is from the documentation, so what does it really mean. It means that Kubernetes will try really hard – and we mean really, really hard – to ensure that the pod and its storage are kept together. One way to help us is also the naming. The pods are named `<pod-name>-#`, where # starts from 0 for the first pod (you know it's a programmer thing).

You can see from the following code that mariadb has a predictable number attached to it, whereas the WordPress Deployment has a random number attached to the end. The numbering reinforces the ephemeral nature of the Deployment pods versus the StatefulSet pods.

```
ab443838-9b3e-4811-b287-74e417a9@Azure:~$ kc get pod
NAME                                          READY     STATUS      RESTARTS
AGE
handsonaks-wp-mariadb-0                        1/1       Running     1
17h
handsonaks-wp-wordpress-6ddcfd5c89-fv6l2       1/1       Running     2
16h
```

Another difference is how pod deletion is handled. When a Deployment Pod is deleted, Kubernetes will launch it again anywhere it can, whereas when a StatefulSet Pod is deleted, Kubernetes will relaunch it only on the node it was running. It will relocate the pod only if the node is removed from Kubernetes cluster.

Another requirement for StatefulSet is dynamically-provisioned persistent volume. Volume can be backed up by many mechanisms (including blocks, such as Azure Blob, EBS, and iSCSI, and network filesystems, such as AFS, NFS, and GlusterFS), please see `https://Kubernetes.io/docs/concepts/storage/volumes/#persistentvolumeclaim` for more information. StatefulSets require dynamically-provisioned volumes handled by PVC. PVC provides an abstraction over the underlying storage mechanism, whether it is backed by block storage or a host directory (not recommended for production use, but works pretty well for local development). Let's look at what the Maria DB helm chart did for us by running the following:

```
kubectl get statefulsets
NAME                      DESIRED   CURRENT   AGE
handsonaks-wp-mariadb     1         1         17h
```

```
kubectl get -o yaml statefulsets/handsonaks-wp-mariadb &gt;
mariadb_statefulset.yaml
code mariadb_statefulset.yaml # open it in the editor
```

For our install, we got the following command:

```
 1 apiVersion: apps/v1
 2 kind: StatefulSet
 3 metadata:
 4   creationTimestamp: 2018-12-27T10:08:51Z
 5   generation: 1
 6   labels:
 7     app: mariadb
 8     chart: mariadb-5.2.5
 9     component: master
10     heritage: Tiller
11     release: handsonaks-wp
12   name: handsonaks-wp-mariadb
13   namespace: default
14   resourceVersion: "182595"
15   selfLink: /apis/apps/v1/namespaces/default/statefulsets/handsonaks-
wp-mariadb
16   uid: 68a51584-09bf-11e9-9914-82000ff4ac53
17 spec:
18   podManagementPolicy: OrderedReady
19   replicas: 1
20   revisionHistoryLimit: 10
21   selector:
22     matchLabels:
23       app: mariadb
24       component: master
25       release: handsonaks-wp
26   serviceName: handsonaks-wp-mariadb
27   template:
28     metadata:
29       creationTimestamp: null
30       labels:
31         app: mariadb
32         chart: mariadb-5.2.5
33         component: master
34         release: handsonaks-wp
35     spec:
36       affinity:
37         podAntiAffinity:
38           preferredDuringSchedulingIgnoredDuringExecution:
39           - podAffinityTerm:
40               labelSelector:
41                 matchLabels:
```

```
42              app: mariadb
43              release: handsonaks-wp
44            topologyKey: Kubernetes .io/hostname
45          weight: 1
46      containers:
47      - env:
48        - name: MARIADB_ROOT_PASSWORD
49          valueFrom:
50            secretKeyRef:
51              key: mariadb-root-password
52              name: handsonaks-wp-mariadb
53        - name: MARIADB_USER
54          value: bn_wordpress
55        - name: MARIADB_PASSWORD
56          valueFrom:
57            secretKeyRef:
58              key: mariadb-password
59              name: handsonaks-wp-mariadb
60        - name: MARIADB_DATABASE
61          value: bitnami_wordpress
62        image: docker.io/bitnami/mariadb:10.1.37
63        imagePullPolicy: IfNotPresent
64        livenessProbe:
65          exec:
66            command:
67            - sh
68            - -c
69            - exec mysqladmin status -uroot -p$MARIADB_ROOT_PASSWORD
70          failureThreshold: 3
71          initialDelaySeconds: 120
72          periodSeconds: 10
73          successThreshold: 1
74          timeoutSeconds: 1
75        name: mariadb
76        ports:
77        - containerPort: 3306
78          name: mysql
79          protocol: TCP
80        readinessProbe:
81          exec:
82            command:
83            - sh
84            - -c
85            - exec mysqladmin status -uroot -p$MARIADB_ROOT_PASSWORD
86          failureThreshold: 3
87          initialDelaySeconds: 30
88          periodSeconds: 10
89          successThreshold: 1
```

```
 90              timeoutSeconds: 1
 91            resources: {}
 92            terminationMessagePath: /dev/termination-log
 93            terminationMessagePolicy: File
 94            volumeMounts:
 95            - mountPath: /bitnami/mariadb
 96              name: data
 97            - mountPath: /opt/bitnami/mariadb/conf/my.cnf
 98              name: config
 99              subPath: my.cnf
100          dnsPolicy: ClusterFirst
101          restartPolicy: Always
102          schedulerName: default-scheduler
103          securityContext:
104            fsGroup: 1001
105            runAsUser: 1001
106          terminationGracePeriodSeconds: 30
107          volumes:
108          - configMap:
109              defaultMode: 420
110              name: handsonaks-wp-mariadb
111            name: config
112    updateStrategy:
113      type: RollingUpdate
114    volumeClaimTemplates:
115    - metadata:
116        creationTimestamp: null
117        labels:
118          app: mariadb
119          component: master
120          heritage: Tiller
121          release: handsonaks-wp
122        name: data
123      spec:
124        accessModes:
125        - ReadWriteOnce
126        resources:
127          requests:
128            storage: 8Gi
129      status:
130        phase: Pending
131  status:
132    collisionCount: 0
133    currentReplicas: 1
134    currentRevision: handsonaks-wp-mariadb-544cbd7968
135    observedGeneration: 1
136    readyReplicas: 1
137    replicas: 1
```

```
138    updateRevision: handsonaks-wp-mariadb-544cbd7968
139    updatedReplicas: 1
```

Those are lots of lines, and if you read them carefully, you will see it is mostly the same information that we provided for Deployment. In the following block, we will highlight the key differences, to take a look at just the PVC:

```
  1 apiVersion: apps/v1
  2 kind: StatefulSet
...
 19    replicas: 1
...
 94         volumeMounts:
 95         - mountPath: /bitnami/mariadb
 96           name: data
...
114    volumeClaimTemplates:
115    - metadata:
117        labels:
118          app: mariadb
119          component: master
120          heritage: Tiller
121          release: handsonaks-wp
122        name: data
123      spec:
124        accessModes:
125        - ReadWriteOnce
126        resources:
127          requests:
128            storage: 8Gi
```

 Persistent Volume Claims (**PVC**) can be used by any Pod, not just StatefulSet Pods.

The following lines will give a detailed explanation of the preceding code:

- **Line 2**: StatefulSet declaration
- **Line 19**: As a Maria/MySQL DB, they don't support running active/inactive multiple instances (unlike Hadoop, for example)
- **Line 94-96**: Mount the volume defined as **data** and mount it under the /bitnami/mariadb path
- **Line 114-122**: Declare the metadata from the volume claim with the **data** ID
- **Line 128**: The size requested for the database storage is 8 Gigabytes

Based on the preceding information, Kubernetes dynamically requests and binds 8Gi volume to this pod. In this case, the default dynamic-storage provisioner backed by Azure Disk is used. The dynamic provisioner is set up by Azure when we created the cluster as shown in the following command and the obtained output:

```
ab443838-9b3e-4811-b287-74e417a9@Azure:~$ kc get storageclass
NAME                     PROVISIONER                AGE
default (default)        Kubernetes .io/azure-disk  8h
managed-premium          Kubernetes .io/azure-disk  2d
```

We get more details about the PVC by running the following:

```
ab443838-9b3e-4811-b287-74e417a9@Azure:~$ kc get pvc
NAME                            STATUS     VOLUME
CAPACITY    ACCESS MODES    STORAGECLASS    AGE
data-handsonaks-wp-mariadb-0    Bound
pvc-68aa2ba4-09bf-11e9-9914-82000ff4ac53    8Gi        RWO
default      19h
```

When we asked for storage in the StatefulSet description (Line 114-128), Kubernetes performed Azure-Disk-specific operations to get the Azure Disk with 8GiB storage:

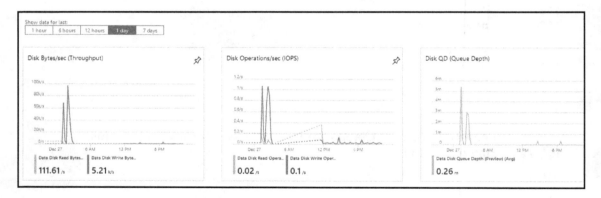

The helm chart keeps the deployment cloud provider agnostic through the use of abstractions, such as PVC. This script would work the same on AWS or GCP. On AWS, it will be backed by EBS, and on GCP it would be Persistent Disk.

Also note that PVC can be deployed without using Helm.

Your own WordPress site

Blogging has enabled Tim Berners Lee's vision of the two-way web. It enables anyone to express their views and knowledge to the whole wide world. Launching and maintaining blogs used to be hard until Kubernetes came along. Remember how you wanted to launch your own blog when you were a kid? Here we are going to make it happen:

```
ab443838-9b3e-4811-b287-74e417a9@Azure:~$ kubectl get svc
NAME                     TYPE           CLUSTER-IP      EXTERNAL-IP
PORT(S)                  AGE
handsonaks-wp-mariadb    ClusterIP      10.0.44.146     <none>
3306/TCP                 21h
handsonaks-wp-wordpress  LoadBalancer   10.0.40.39      52.183.78.32
80:31044/TCP,443:32007/TCP   21h
Kubernetes               ClusterIP      10.0.0.1        <none>
443/TCP                  2d
```

Go to http://<external-ip-shown>:

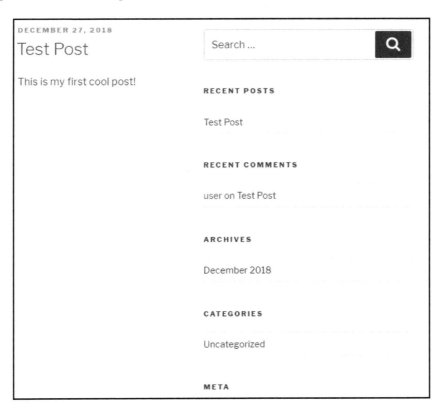

To delete the WordPress site, run the following:

```
helm delete --purge handsonaks-wp
```

Summary

This chapter was the big one. We went from a simple Docker container mapped to a Pod, to Pods running as ReplicaSet, to ReplicaSets under Deployment, to StatefulSets managing **Persistent Volume Claims** (**PVCs**). We went from launching using raw Kubernetes `yaml` files to installing complex applications using Helm charts.

In the next chapter, you will learn how to perform cool tricks, such as scaling your application, and what to do when things go wrong. The power of the Kubernetes declarative engine, which lets you specify the desired state and let the machine figure out how to achieve it, will be realized. Without having advanced Network certification or knowledge, you will be able to diagnose common network errors while troubleshooting Kubernetes applications.

4

Scaling Your Application to Thousands of Deployments

In this chapter, we will show you how to scale the sample application that we introduced in Chapter 2, *Kubernetes on Azure (AKS)*, using kubectl. We will introduce different failures to demonstrate the power of Kubernetes' declarative engine. The goal is to make you comfortable with kubectl, which is an important tool for managing AKS. In addition, in this chapter you will get a brief introduction to how network traffic is routed to different pods running on different nodes, and how it will help you to diagnose network problems in production.

In this chapter, we'll cover the following topics:

- Scaling your application
- Handling failure in AKS
- Upgrading your application

Technical requirements

For this chapter, you will need any modern browser, such as Chrome, Firefox, Safari, or Edge.

You will find the code files for this chapter by accessing https://github.com/ PacktPublishing/Hands-On-Kubernetes-on-Azure.

Scaling your application

Scaling on demand is one of the key benefits of using cloud-native applications. It also helps optimize resources for your application. If the frontend component encounters heavy loads, you can scale the frontend alone, while keeping the same number of backend instances. You can increase or reduce the number/size of VMs required depending on your workload and peak demand hours. You will scale your application components independently and also see how to troubleshoot scaling issues.

Implementing independent scaling

To demonstrate independent scaling, let's use the guestbook example that we used in the previous chapter. Let's follow these steps to learn how to implement independent scaling:

1. Install the guestbook by running the `kubectl create` command in the Azure command line:

   ```
   kubectl create -f
   https://raw.githubusercontent.com/kubernetes/examples/master/guestb
   ook/all-in-one/guestbook-all-in-one.yaml
   ```

2. After you have entered the preceding command, you should see the following output in your command-line output:

   ```
   ab443838-9b3e-4811-b287-74e417a9@Azure:~$ kubectl create -f
   https://raw.githubusercontent.com/kubernetes/examples/master/guestb
   ook/all-in-one/guestbook-all-in-one.yaml
   service/redis-master created
   deployment.apps/redis-master created
   service/redis-slave created
   deployment.apps/redis-slave created
   service/frontend created
   deployment.apps/frontend created
   ```

3. After a few minutes, you should get the following output in which you will see that none of the containers are accessible from the internet, and no external IP is assigned:

   ```
   ab443838-9b3e-4811-b287-74e417a9@Azure:~$ kc get all
   NAME READY STATUS RESTARTS AGE
   pod/frontend-56f7975f44-7sdn5 1/1 Running 0 1m
   pod/frontend-56f7975f44-hscn7 1/1 Running 0 1m
   pod/frontend-56f7975f44-pqvbg 1/1 Running 0 1m
   ```

```
pod/redis-master-6b464554c8-8nv4s 1/1 Running 0 1m
pod/redis-slave-b58dc4644-597qt 1/1 Running 0 1m
pod/redis-slave-b58dc4644-xtdkx 1/1 Running 0 1m

NAME TYPE CLUSTER-IP EXTERNAL-IP PORT(S) AGE
service/frontend ClusterIP 10.0.174.190 <none> 80/TCP 1m
service/kubernetes ClusterIP 10.0.0.1 <none> 443/TCP 3d
service/redis-master ClusterIP 10.0.208.204 <none> 6379/TCP 1m
service/redis-slave ClusterIP 10.0.225.59 <none> 6379/TCP 1m

NAME DESIRED CURRENT UP-TO-DATE AVAILABLE AGE
deployment.apps/frontend 3 3 3 3 1m
deployment.apps/redis-master 1 1 1 1 1m
deployment.apps/redis-slave 2 2 2 2 1m

NAME DESIRED CURRENT READY AGE
replicaset.apps/frontend-56f7975f44 3 3 3 1m
replicaset.apps/redis-master-6b464554c8 1 1 1 1m
replicaset.apps/redis-slave-b58dc4644 2 2 2 1m
```

4. Expose the frontend to the public internet by default using the following command:

```
kc get -o yaml svc/frontend > frontend-service.yaml
code frontend-service.yaml
```

5. Edit the frontend-service.yaml file to set the labels, ports, and selector, which should appear as follows (or you can cut and paste the following):

```
apiVersion: v1
kind: Service
metadata:
 labels:
 app: guestbook
 tier: frontend
 name: frontend
spec:
 ports:
 - port: 80
 protocol: TCP
 targetPort: 80
 selector:
 app: guestbook
 tier: frontend
 type: LoadBalancer
```

6. Save the file and recreate the frontend service so that we can access it publicly by deleting the frontend service and recreating it as follows:

```
kubectl delete -f frontend-service.yaml
kubectl create -f frontend-service.yaml
```

7. Use the following command to get the public IP to access the application via the internet:

```
kubectl get svc
```

You will get the following output. You need to look for the IP displayed under the EXTERNAL-IP column:

NAME	TYPE	CLUSTER-IP	EXTERNAL-IP
PORT(S)	AGE		
frontend	LoadBalancer	10.0.196.116	<EXTERNAL-IP>
80:30063/TCP	2m		

8. Type the IP address from the preceding output into your browser navigation bar as follows: http://<EXTERNAL-IP>/. The result of this is shown in the following screenshot:

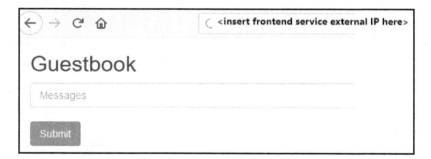

The familiar guestbook sample should be visible. You have successfully publically accessed the guestbook.

Scaling the guestbook frontend component

Kubernetes gives us the ability to scale each component of an application dynamically. In this section, we will show you how to scale the frontend of the guestbook application as follows:

```
ab443838-9b3e-4811-b287-74e417a9@Azure:~$ kc scale --replicas=6
deployment/frontend
deployment.extensions/frontend scaled
ab443838-9b3e-4811-b287-74e417a9@Azure:~$ kc get all
NAME                              READY     STATUS            RESTARTS
AGE
pod/frontend-56f7975f44-2rnst     1/1       Running           0
4s
pod/frontend-56f7975f44-4tgkm     1/1       Running           0
4s
pod/frontend-56f7975f44-7sdn5     1/1       Running           0
2h
pod/frontend-56f7975f44-hscn7     1/1       Running           0
2h
pod/frontend-56f7975f44-p2k9w     0/1       ContainerCreating 0
4s
pod/frontend-56f7975f44-pqvbg     1/1       Running           0
2h
```

We achieve this by using the `scale` option in `kubectl`. You can set the number of replicas you want, and Kubernetes takes care of the rest. You can even scale it down to zero (one of the tricks used to reload configuration when the application doesn't support the dynamic reload of configuration). You can see this trick in action as follows:

```
ab443838-9b3e-4811-b287-74e417a9@Azure:~$ kc scale --replicas=0
deployment/frontend
deployment.extensions/frontend scaled
ab443838-9b3e-4811-b287-74e417a9@Azure:~$ kc get pods
NAME                         READY   STATUS        RESTARTS   AGE
frontend-56f7975f44-4vh7c    0/1     Terminating   0          3m
frontend-56f7975f44-75trq    0/1     Terminating   0          3m
frontend-56f7975f44-p6ht5    0/1     Terminating   0          3m
frontend-56f7975f44-pqvbg    0/1     Terminating   1          14h
```

Let's bring it back to 3 replicas from 0 by using the following command:

```
ab443838-9b3e-4811-b287-74e417a9@Azure:~$ kc scale --replicas=3
deployment/frontend
deployment.extensions/frontend scaled
```

In this chapter, you have experienced how easy it is to scale pods with Kubernetes. This capability provides a very powerful tool for you to not only dynamically adjust your application components, but also to provide resilient applications with failover capabilities enabled by running multiple instances of components at the same time.

Furthermore, its declarative nature is another key advantage of using Kubernetes. In the previous examples, we saw that we need to define what we want (namely, the number of the replicas) in the .yaml file description, and Kubernetes handles the rest.

Besides the number of replicas, we can define other components in a descriptive way, some of which are given here:

- Desired versus available nodes (if they are the same, take no action)
- The number of pods
- Pod placement based on CPU/memory requirements
- The handling of special cases such as StatefulSets

Handling failure in AKS

Kubernetes is a distributed system with many hidden working parts. AKS abstracts all of it for us, but it is still our responsibility to know where to look and how to respond when bad things happen. Much of the failure handling is done automatically by Kubernetes – still, you will run into situations where manual intervention is required. The following is a list of the most common failure modes that require interaction. We will look into the following failure modes in depth in this section:

- Node failures
- Out-of-resource failure
- Storage mount issues
- Network issues

See Kubernetes the Hard Way (https://github.com/kelseyhightower/kubernetes-the-hard-way), an excellent tutorial, to get an idea about the blocks on which Kubernetes is built. For the Azure version, see *Kubernetes the Hard Way – Azure Translation* (https://github.com/ivanfioravanti/kubernetes-the-hard-way-on-azure).

Node failures

Intentionally (to save costs) or unintentionally, nodes can go down. When that happens, you don't want to get the proverbial 3AM call when Kubernetes can handle it automatically for you instead. In this exercise, we are going to bring a node down in our cluster and see what Kubernetes does in response:

1. Ensure that your cluster has at least two nodes:

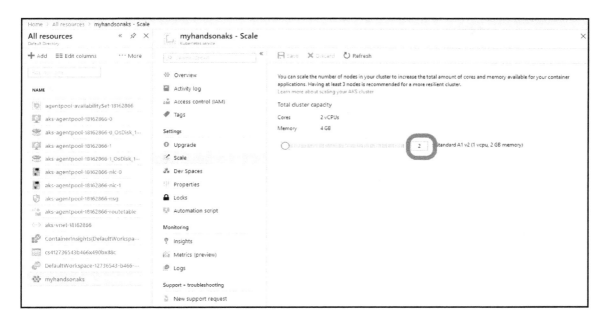

2. Check that your URL is working as shown in the following output, using the external IP to reach the frontend:

```
kc get svc
NAME            TYPE           CLUSTER-IP      EXTERNAL-IP
PORT(S)         AGE
frontend        LoadBalancer   10.0.196.116    EXTERNAL-IP
80:30063/TCP    14h
```

3. Go to `http://<EXTERNAL-IP>`:

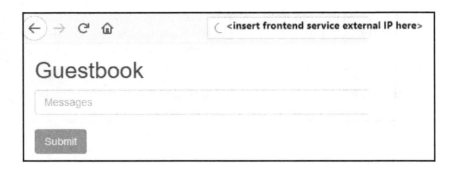

4. Let's see where the pods are running currently using the following code:

```
kubectl describe nodes
```

The following output is edited to show only the lines we are interested in:

```
 1 ab443838-9b3e-4811-b287-74e417a9@Azure:~$ kc describe nodes
 2 Name:                    aks-agentpool-18162866-0
 5 Addresses:
 6    InternalIP:   10.240.0.4
 7 Hostname: aks-agentpool-18162866-0
16 Non-terminated Pods:          (12 in total)
17    Namespace                    Name                          CPU
Requests  CPU Limits  Memory Requests  Memory Limits
18    ---------                    ----                          -------
-----   ----------   ---------------   --------------
19    default                      frontend-56f7975f44-9k7f2     100m
(10%)    0 (0%)     100Mi (7%)      0 (0%)
20    default                      frontend-56f7975f44-rflgz     100m
(10%)    0 (0%)     100Mi (7%)      0 (0%)
21    default                      redis-master-6b464554c8-8nv4s 100m
(10%)    0 (0%)     100Mi (7%)      0 (0%)
22    default                      redis-slave-b58dc4644-wtkwj   100m
(10%)    0 (0%)     100Mi (7%)      0 (0%)
23    default                      redis-slave-b58dc4644-xtdkx   100m
(10%)    0 (0%)     100Mi (7%)      0 (0%)
39 Name:               aks-agentpool-18162866-1
42 Addresses:
43    InternalIP:   10.240.0.5
44    Hostname:     aks-agentpool-18162866-1
54    Namespace                    Name
CPU Requests  CPU Limits  Memory Requests  Memory Limits
55    ---------                    ----
-----------   ----------   ---------------   -------------                  -
```

```
56    default                      frontend-56f7975f44-gbsfv
100m (10%)     0 (0%)         100Mi (7%)       0 (0%)
```

We can see that on `agent-0`, we have the following:

- Two frontend servers (out of three)
- One redis master
- Two redis slaves

On `agent-1`, we have the following:

- One frontend server

5. In this case, we are going for maximum damage, so let's shut down `agent-0` (you can choose whichever node you want – for illustration purposes, it doesn't really matter):

Let the fun begin.

6. For maximum fun, you can run the following command to hit the guestbook frontend every 5 seconds and return the HTML (on any Bash Terminal):

```
while true; do curl http://<EXTERNAl-IP>/ ; sleep 5; done
```

The preceding command will generate infinite scroll till you press *Ctrl + C*.

Add some Guestbook entries to see what happens to them when you cause the node to shut down.

Things will go crazy during the shutdown of `agent-0`. You can see this in the following edited output generated during the shutdown:

```
ab443838-9b3e-4811-b287-74e417a9@Azure:~$ kc get events --watch
LAST SEEN FIRST SEEN COUNT NAME KIND SUBOBJECT TYPE REASON SOURCE MESSAGE
47m 47m 1 frontend-56f7975f44-9k7f2.1574e5f94ac87d7c Pod Normal Scheduled
default-scheduler Successfully assigned default/frontend-56f7975f44-9k7f2
to aks-agentpool-18162866-0
47m 47m 1 frontend-56f7975f44-9k7f2.1574e5f9c9eb2713 Pod
spec.containers{php-redis} Normal Pulled kubelet, aks-agentpool-18162866-0
Container image "gcr.io/google-samples/gb-frontend:v4" already present on
machine
47m 47m 1 frontend-56f7975f44-9k7f2.1574e5f9e3ee2348 Pod
spec.containers{php-redis} Normal Created kubelet, aks-agentpool-18162866-0
Created container
47m 47m 1 frontend-56f7975f44-9k7f2.1574e5fa0ec58afa Pod
spec.containers{php-redis} Normal Started kubelet, aks-agentpool-18162866-0
Started container
52s 52s 1 frontend-56f7975f44-fbksv.1574e88a6e05a7eb Pod Normal Scheduled
default-scheduler Successfully assigned default/frontend-56f7975f44-fbksv
to aks-agentpool-18162866-1
50s 50s 1 frontend-56f7975f44-fbksv.1574e88aec0fb81d Pod
spec.containers{php-redis} Normal Pulled kubelet, aks-agentpool-18162866-0
Container image "gcr.io/google-samples/gb-frontend:v4" already present on
machine
47m 47m 1 frontend-56f7975f44-rflgz.1574e5f9e7166672 Pod
spec.containers{php-redis} Normal Created kubelet, aks-agentpool-18162866-0
Created container
47m 47m 1 frontend-56f7975f44-rflgz.1574e5fa1524773e Pod
spec.containers{php-redis} Normal Started kubelet, aks-agentpool-18162866-0
Started container
52s 52s 1 frontend-56f7975f44-xw7vd.1574e88a716fa558 Pod Normal Scheduled
default-scheduler Successfully assigned default/frontend-56f7975f44-xw7vd
to aks-agentpool-18162866-1
49s 49s 1 frontend-56f7975f44-xw7vd.1574e88b37cf57f1 Pod
spec.containers{php-redis} Normal Pulled kubelet, aks-agentpool-18162866-1
Container image "gcr.io/google-samples/gb-frontend:v4" already present on
machine
48s 48s 1 frontend-56f7975f44-xw7vd.1574e88b4cb8959f Pod
spec.containers{php-redis} Normal Created kubelet, aks-agentpool-18162866-1
Created container
47s 47s 1 frontend-56f7975f44-xw7vd.1574e88b8aee5ee6 Pod
spec.containers{php-redis} Normal Started kubelet, aks-agentpool-18162866-1
Started container
47m 47m 1 frontend-56f7975f44.1574e5f9483ea97c ReplicaSet Normal
```

```
SuccessfulCreate replicaset-controller Created pod: frontend-56f7975f44-
gbsfv
47m 47m 1 frontend-56f7975f44.1574e5f949bd8e43 ReplicaSet Normal
SuccessfulCreate replicaset-
8s 52s 8 redis-master-6b464554c8-f5p7f.1574e88a71687da6 Pod Warning
FailedScheduling default-scheduler 0/2 nodes are available: 1 Insufficient
cpu, 1 node(s) were not ready, 1 node(s) were out of disk space.
52s 52s 1 redis-master-6b464554c8.1574e88a716d02d9 ReplicaSet Normal
SuccessfulCreate replicaset-controller Created pod: redis-
master-6b464554c8-f5p7f
8s 52s 7 redis-slave-b58dc4644-7w468.1574e88a73b5ecc4 Pod Warning
FailedScheduling default-scheduler 0/2 nodes are available: 1 Insufficient
cpu, 1 node(s) were not ready, 1 node(s) were out of disk space.
8s 52s 8 redis-slave-b58dc4644-lqkdp.1574e88a78913f1a Pod Warning
FailedScheduling default-scheduler 0/2 nodes are available: 1 Insufficient
cpu, 1 node(s) were not ready, 1 node(s) were out of disk space.
52s 52s 1 redis-slave-b58dc4644.1574e88a73b40e64 ReplicaSet Normal
SuccessfulCreate replicaset-controller Created pod: redis-slave-
b58dc4644-7w468
52s 52s 1 redis-slave-b58dc4644.1574e88a78901fd9 ReplicaSet Normal
SuccessfulCreate replicaset-controller Created pod: redis-slave-b58dc4644-
lqkdp
0s 54s 8 redis-slave-b58dc4644-7w468.1574e88a73b5ecc4 Pod Warning
FailedScheduling default-scheduler 0/2 nodes are available: 1 Insufficient
cpu, 1 node(s) were not ready, 1 node(s) were out of disk space.
0s 54s 9 redis-slave-b58dc4644-lqkdp.1574e88a78913f1a Pod Warning
FailedScheduling default-scheduler 0/2 nodes are available: 1 Insufficient
cpu, 1 node(s) were not ready, 1 node(s) were out of disk space.
0s 54s 9 redis-master-6b464554c8-f5p7f.1574e88a71687da6 Pod
0s 1m 13 redis-slave-b58dc4644-lqkdp.1574e88a78913f1a Pod Warning
FailedScheduling default-scheduler 0/2 nodes are available: 1 Insufficient
cpu, 1 node(s) were not ready, 1 node(s) were out of disk space.
```

Take a look at the guestbook application in the browser:

What you can see is that all your precious messages are gone! This shows the importance of having **Persistent Volume Claims** (**PVCs**) for any data that you want to survive in the case of a node failure.

Let's look at some messages from the frontend and understand what they mean:

```
9m 1h 3 frontend.1574e31070390293 Service Normal UpdatedLoadBalancer
service-controller                       Updated load balancer with new hosts
```

The preceding message is the first hint we get when something goes wrong. Your curl command might have hiccupped a little bit, but has continued. You have to hit the frontend URL on your browser for migration to kick in. The reason you have to reload the frontend is because of how the frontend is that constructed, it just loads the HTML and expects JavaScript to hit the Redis database. So, hit refresh on your browser:

```
52s             52s                1               frontend-56f7975f44-
fbksv.1574e88a6e05a7eb          Pod
Normal      Scheduled                  default-scheduler
Successfully assigned default/frontend-56f7975f44-fbksv to aks-
agentpool-18162866-1
```

You can see that one of the frontend pods is scheduled for migration to `agent-1`:

```
50s             50s                1               frontend-56f7975f44-
fbksv.1574e88aec0fb81d          Pod             spec.containers{php-redis}
Normal      Pulled                     kubelet, aks-agentpool-18162866-1
Container image "gcr.io/google-samples/gb-frontend:v4" already present on
machine
50s             50s                1               frontend-56f7975f44-
fbksv.1574e88b004c01e6          Pod             spec.containers{php-redis}
Normal      Created                    kubelet, aks-agentpool-18162866-1    Created
container
49s             49s                1               frontend-56f7975f44-
fbksv.1574e88b44244673          Pod             spec.containers{php-redis}
Normal      Started                    kubelet, aks-agentpool-18162866-1    Started
container
```

Next, Kubernetes checks whether the Docker image is present on the node and downloads it if required. Furthermore, the container is created and started.

Diagnosing out-of-resource errors

When deleting `agent-0`, we can observe the issue of being out of resources. Only one node is available, but that node is out of disk space:

```
0s           1m          13          redis-slave-b58dc4644-1qkdp.1574e88a78913f1a
Pod                      Warning     FailedScheduling    default-scheduler    0/2
nodes are available: 1 Insufficient cpu, 1 node(s) were not ready, 1
node(s) were out of disk space.
```

To confirm this, run the following command:

```
kc get pods
```

When you run the command, you will get the following output:

```
redis-slave-b58dc4644-tcl2x      0/1      Pending    0          4h
redis-slave-b58dc4644-wtkwj      1/1      Unknown    0          6h
redis-slave-b58dc4644-xtdkx      1/1      Unknown    1          20h
```

 If you had launched the cluster on VMs with more vCPUs (ours was running the smallest available, A1), you can set the replicas to be 10 or higher to recreate this issue as follows:
`kubectl scale --replicas=10 deployment/redis-slave`

Now that we have confirmed the issue, let's get back to the error:

```
redis-slave-... Warning   FailedScheduling ...    0/2 nodes are available: 1
Insufficient cpu, 1 node(s) were not ready, 1 node(s) were out of disk
space.
```

There are three errors as follows:

- Insufficient CPU
- One node not ready
- One node out of disk space

Let's look at them in detail:

- **One node not ready**: We know about this error because we caused it. We can also probably guess that it is the same node that is reporting out of disk space.

How can we make sure that it is the `Insufficient cpu` issue instead of the node being out of disk space? Let's explore this using the following steps:

1. Get hold of a running pod:

```
kc get pods
NAME                            READY   STATUS    RESTARTS   AGE
frontend-56f7975f44-9k7f2       1/1     Unknown   0          5h
frontend-56f7975f44-1snrq       1/1     Running   0          4h
```

2. Use the `kubectl exec` command to run a shell on the node as follows:

```
kc exec -it frontend-<running-pod-id> bash
```

3. Once we are in, run the following command:

```
df -h
```

The output we should get will be similar to the following:

```
root@frontend-56f7975f44-1snrq:/var/www/html# df -h
Filesystem      Size  Used Avail Use% Mounted on
overlay          30G   15G   15G  51% /
tmpfs            64M     0   64M   0% /dev
tmpfs           966M     0  966M   0% /sys/fs/cgroup
/dev/sda1        30G   15G   15G  51% /etc/hosts
shm              64M     0   64M   0% /dev/shm
tmpfs           966M   12K  965M   1%
/run/secrets/kubernetes.io/serviceaccount
tmpfs           966M     0  966M   0% /proc/acpi
tmpfs           966M     0  966M   0% /proc/scsi
tmpfs           966M     0  966M   0% /sys/firmware
```

4. Clearly there is enough disk space, since the node is not reporting a status. So, enter the following command to know why the node is showing `out of disk space`:

```
kc describe nodes
```

This is not much of help in determining where the `out of disk space` issue is coming from (the `Unknown` status doesn't mean out of disk). This seems to be a bug in the eventing mechanism reporter of Kubernetes, although this bug might be fixed by the time you read this.

In our case, the CPU is the bottleneck. So, let's see what Kubernetes is having trouble with, by getting the `ReplicaSet` definition of `redis-slave` as follows:

```
ab443838-9b3e-4811-b287-74e417a9@Azure:~$ kc get rs
NAME                      DESIRED   CURRENT   READY     AGE
frontend-56f7975f44       1         1         1         20h
redis-master-6b464554c8   1         1         1         20h
redis-slave-b58dc4644     1         1         0         20h
ab443838-9b3e-4811-b287-74e417a9@Azure:~$ kc get -o yaml rs/redis-slave-
b58dc4644
apiVersion: extensions/v1beta1
...
kind: ReplicaSet
        resources:
          requests:
            cpu: 100m
```

You might think that since `redis-slave` is used only for reading, the application might still work. On the surface, it looks okay. The guestbook appears in the browser when we enter the IP address as follows:

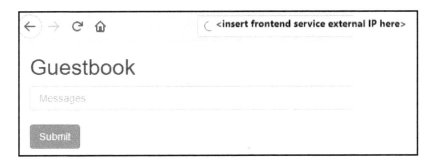

But if you try to add an entry, nothing happens.

The Developer Web Tools are good debugging tools for these cases, and are available in most browsers. You can launch them by right clicking and choosing `Inspect`:

After a page refresh, you can see this error in the **Network** tab:

```
<br />
<b>Fatal error</b>:  Uncaught exception
'Predis\Connection\ConnectionException' with message 'Connection timed out
[tcp://redis-slave:6379]' in
/usr/local/lib/php/Predis/Connection/AbstractConnection.php:168
```

There are multiple ways we can solve this issue. In production, you would restart the node or add additional nodes. To demonstrate, we will try multiple approaches (all of them coming from practical experience).

Reducing the number of replicas to the bare minimum

Our first approach is to reduce the number of replicas to only what is essential by using the following command:

```
ab443838-9b3e-4811-b287-74e417a9@Azure:~$ kc scale --replicas=1
deployment/frontend
deployment.extensions/frontend scaled
ab443838-9b3e-4811-b287-74e417a9@Azure:~$ kc scale --replicas=1
deployment/redis-slave
deployment.extensions/redis-slave scaled
```

Let's check the events as follows:

```
kc get events
LAST SEEN    FIRST SEEN    COUNT    NAME
KIND       SUBOBJECT    TYPE      REASON            SOURCE
MESSAGE
1m          5h            1973      redis-slave-b58dc4644-
tcl2x.1574e9eadbae3e88    Pod                    Warning    FailedScheduling
default-scheduler   0/2 nodes are available: 1 Insufficient cpu, 1 node(s)
were not ready, 1 node(s) were out of disk space.
```

Despite reducing the replicas, we still get the error message. The VM that we are running simply does not have the horsepower to run these apps.

Reducing CPU requirements

We can use the same trick of changing the `yaml` file as we did earlier, as follows:

```
kc get -o yaml deploy/frontend > frontend.yaml
...
```

This time, we are going to download the `yaml` file and modify it as follows:

```
curl -O -L
https://raw.githubusercontent.com/kubernetes/examples/master/guestbook/all-
in-one/guestbook-all-in-one.yaml
```

Find **resources** | **cpu** limit for `redis-slave` and `frontend` and replace `100m` with `10m`:

```
cpu: 10m
```

Remember that the advantage of using Deployments versus plain Replication Controllers was the ability to roll out an upgrade. We can use that capability to let Kubernetes make the required changes in a declarative fashion.

In our case, we get this new error from the `kubectl get events` command:

```
1s          18s              4         redis-slave-b6566c98-
gq5cw.15753462c1fbce76       Pod
Warning   FailedScheduling          default-scheduler     0/2 nodes are
available: 1 Insufficient memory, 1 node(s) were not ready, 1 node(s) were
out of disk space.
```

To fix the error shown in the previous code, let's edit the memory requirements in the `yaml` file as well. This time, we will use the following command:

```
kubectl edit deploy/redis-deploy
```

Change the memory requirement to the following:

```
memory: 10Mi
```

> You have to remember `vi` commands to edit the memory requirements:
>
> - Press *i* to change text
> - Press *Esc* to get out edit mode
> - Then *:wq* to write the file out and quit

Kubernetes makes the required changes to make things happen. Make changes to replicas and resource settings to get to this state:

```
ab443838-9b3e-4811-b287-74e417a9@Azure:~$ kc get pods |grep Running
frontend-84d8dff7c4-98pph         1/1       Running   0          1h
redis-master-6b464554c8-f5p7f     1/1       Running   1          23h
redis-slave-787d9ffb96-wsf62      1/1       Running   0          1m
```

The guestbook appears in the browser when we enter the IP address as follows:

Since we now have the entries, we can confirm that the application is working properly.

Cleanup of the guestbook deployment

Let's clean up by running the following `delete` command:

```
kc delete -f guestbook-all-in-one.yaml
```

Also, restart `node-0` to get to a functioning cluster:

This completes the another most common failure nodes wherein you were able to identify the errors that lead to the issue and fix it.

Fixing storage mount issues

In this section, you will fix the issue we experienced earlier in this chapter of non-persistent storage if a node goes down. Before we start, let's make sure that the cluster is in a clean state:

```
ab443838-9b3e-4811-b287-74e417a9@Azure:~$ kc get all
NAME                 TYPE        CLUSTER-IP   EXTERNAL-IP   PORT(S)   AGE
service/kubernetes   ClusterIP   10.0.0.1     <none>        443/TCP   4d
```

Get the status of running nodes:

```
ab443838-9b3e-4811-b287-74e417a9@Azure:~$ kc get nodes
NAME                      STATUS   ROLES   AGE   VERSION
aks-agentpool-18162866-0  Ready    agent   4d    v1.11.5
aks-agentpool-18162866-1  Ready    agent   3d    v1.11.5
```

In the last example, we saw that the messages stored in `redis-master` were lost if it gets restarted. The reason for this is that `redis-master` stores all data in its container, and whenever it is restarted, it uses the clean image without the data. In order to survive reboots, the data has to be stored *outside*. Kubernetes uses PVCs to abstract the underlying storage provider to provide this external storage.

Starting the WordPress install

Let's start by reinstalling WordPress. We will show how it works and then verify that storage is still present after a reboot:

1. Start reinstalling using the following command:

   ```
   helm install stable/wordpress --name handsonaks-wp
   ```

2. At the time of writing, the preceding command didn't work. We debugged the error by running the following code:

   ```
   kubectl logs pod/cantankerous-buffoon-wordpress-<rs-id>-<pod-id>
   ```

3. This gives us the following error:

   ```
   Error executing 'postInstallation': You should specify username,
   password, host, port for SMTP configuration
   ```

   This error showed that some bug in the script was expecting that the SMTP variables would be set (in theory, you are allowed to set it as empty).

4. To work around the issue, run the `helm` command as follows:

   ```
   helm delete --purge handsonaks-wp
   kc delete pvc/data-handsonaks-wp-mariadb-0
   helm install stable/wordpress --name handsonaks-wp --set
   smtpHost=smtp.google.com --set smtpPort=25 --set
   smtpPassword=abcd1234 --set smtpUser=handsonaks@gmail.com --set
   smtpUsername=handsonaks --set smtpProtocol=ssl
   ```

   This will take a couple of minutes to process.

Persistent volumes

Let's explore persistent volumes (PVs):

1. In our case, run the following `describe nodes` command:

```
kc describe nodes
```

The preceding command gives the following output:

```
Namespace Name  CPU Requests  CPU Limits  Memory Requests  Memory Limits
  default   handsonaks-wp-mariadb-0                         0 (0%)          0
(0%)      0 (0%)          0 (0%)
  default   handsonaks-wp-wordpress-6ddcfd5c89-p2925    300m (31%)      0
(0%)      512Mi (38%)      0 (0%)
```

2. Are all pods on `agent-0`? Your pod placement may vary. To verify this run the following command:

```
ab443838-9b3e-4811-b287-74e417a9@Azure:~$ kc get pvc
NAME                     STATUS    VOLUME                    CAPACITY   ACCESS
MODES    STORAGECLASS   AGE
data-handsonaks-wp-mariadb-0    Bound
pvc-752cea13-0c73-11e9-9914-82000ff4ac53   8Gi  RWO  default 1h
handsonaks-wp-wordpress            Bound
pvc-74f785bc-0c73-11e9-9914-82000ff4ac53   10Gi  RWO default 1h
```

The following command shows the PVCs that are bound to the pods:

```
kc get pv # the actual persistent volumes
...
Type:         AzureDisk (an Azure Data Disk mount on the host and bind
mount to the pod)
    DiskName:     kubernetes-dynamic-
pvc-74f785bc-0c73-11e9-9914-82000ff4ac53
    DiskURI:        /subscriptions/12736543-b466-490b-88c6-
f1136a239821/resourceGroups/MC_cloud-shell-storage-
westus_myhandsonaks_westus2/providers/Microsoft.Compute/disks/kubernetes-
dynamic-pvc-74f785bc-0c73-11e9-9914-82000ff4ac53
...
# shows the actual disk backing up the PVC
```

3. Verify that your site is actually working:

```
ab443838-9b3e-4811-b287-74e417a9@Azure:~$ kc get svc
NAME                       TYPE          CLUSTER-IP     EXTERNAL-IP
PORT(S)                    AGE
handsonaks-wp-wordpress    LoadBalancer  10.0.78.128    <EXTERNAL-IP>
80:31425/TCP,443:31446/TCP  1h
```

4. Log on to the site (using the **Log In** link) as follows:

```
helm status handsonaks-wp
echo Password: $(kubectl get secret --namespace default handsonaks-wp-
wordpress -o jsonpath="{.data.wordpress-password}" | base64 --decode)
```

5. Add a test post and click on **Post Comment** to publish it:

We will verify whether this post survives a reboot in the next section.

Handling node failure with PVC involvement

Let's run the `describe nodes` command again as follows:

```
kubectl describe nodes
```

We found that, in our cluster, `agent-0` had all the critical pods of the database and WordPress.

We are going to be evil again and stop the node that can cause most damage by shutting down `node-0` on the Azure portal:

Let the fun begin.

Click refresh on the page to verify that the page does not work.

You have to wait at least 300s (in this case) as that is the default for Kubernetes for `tolerations`. Check this by running the following command:

```
kc describe pods/<pod-id>
```

You will get the following output:

```
Tolerations:        node.kubernetes.io/not-ready:NoExecute for 300s
                    node.kubernetes.io/unreachable:NoExecute for 300s
```

Keep refreshing the page once in a while, and eventually you will see Kubernetes try to migrate the pod to the running agent.

Use `kubectl edit deploy/...` to fix any insufficient CPU/memory errors as shown in the last section.

In our case, we see these errors when you run `kubectl get events`:

```
2s            2s            1          handsonaks-wp-wordpress-55644f585c-
hqmn5.15753d7898e1545c    Pod                        Warning
FailedAttachVolume    attachdetach-controller    Multi-Attach error for
volume "pvc-74f785bc-0c73-11e9-9914-82000ff4ac53" Volume is already used by
pod(s) handsonaks-wp-wordpress-6ddcfd5c89-p2925
36s           36s           1          handsonaks-wp-wordpress-55644f585c-
hqmn5.15753d953ce0bdca    Pod                        Warning    FailedMount
kubelet, aks-agentpool-18162866-1    Unable to mount volumes for pod
"handsonaks-wp-wordpress-55644f585c-
hqmn5_default(ec03818d-0c83-11e9-9914-82000ff4ac53)": timeout expired
waiting for volumes to attach or mount for pod "default"/"handsonaks-wp-
wordpress-55644f585c-hqmn5". list of unmounted volumes=[wordpress-data].
list of unattached volumes=[wordpress-data default-token-rskvs]
a
```

This is because storage detachment from a VM is a tricky business, and Azure has a high tolerance before it would let you detach storage from one VM. As usual, there are multiple ways around this issue:

- Use the Azure portal to manually detach the disk we identified previously.
- Delete the old pod manually (the one with the status Unknown) to force-detach the volume.
- Give it around 5 or 10 minutes, then delete the pod to force Kubernetes to try again.

By trying some, or all, of these, we were able to mount the WordPress volume on `agent-1`, but not the `mariadb` volume. We had to restart `agent-0` to get the cluster to a decent state. At this point, there are only two options:

- Get Microsoft support.
- Make sure that you have good backup.

It is for this reason and more that we recommend using managed DBs for your pods and not hosting them yourself. We will see how we can do that in the upcoming chapters.

When your cluster is running for a long time, or at scale, eventually you will run into the following issues:

- The kube DNS kubelet stops working and will require a restart.
- Azure limits outside connections from a single VM to 1,024.
- If any of your pods create zombie processes and don't clean up, you won't be able to even connect to the pod. You will have to restart the pod.

Before continuing, let's clean up the PV/PVC using the following command:

```
helm delete --purge handsonaks-wp
# delete any pv or pvc that might be present using kubectl delete pvc/...
```

By the end of this section, you now have a detailed knowledge in studying and fixing node failures.

Upgrading your application

Using Deployments makes upgrading a straightforward operation. As with any upgrade, you should have good backups in case something goes wrong. Most of the issues you will run into will happen during upgrades. Cloud-native applications are supposed to make dealing with this relatively easier which is possible only if you have a very strong development team that has the ability to do incremental rollouts (with support for rollback).

There is a trade-off between getting features out for customers to see versus spending a lot of time ensuring developer training, automated tests, and disciplined developers and product managers. Remember, most successful companies that do upgrades in production multiple times a day had for years monolithic applications that generated revenue before they were able to switch to a microservices-based approach.

Most methods here work great if you have stateless applications. If you have a state stored anywhere, back up before you try anything.

kubectl edit

For a deployment, all we have to do is change the values that we want to change using the `kubectl edit` command as follows:

```
kubectl edit <resource>
```

The deployment detects the changes (if any) and matches the running state to the desired state. Lets see how its done:

1. We start with our guestbook application to demonstrate this example:

```
curl -O -L
https://raw.githubusercontent.com/kubernetes/examples/master/guestbook/all-
in-one/guestbook-all-in-one.yaml
kubectl create -f guestbook-all-in-one.yaml
```

2. After few minutes, all the pods should be running. Let's do our first upgrade by changing the service from `ClusterIP` to `LoadBalancer`:

```
code guestbook-all-in-one.yaml
#change the frontend service section from ClusterIP to LoadBalancer
# refer the previous sections if you are not sure how to change it
```

3. Apply the change as shown in the following code:

```
kubectl apply -f guestbook-all-in-one.yaml
```

4. You should see the external IP pending message (you can ignore the warnings about using the `saveconfig` option):

```
ab443838-9b3e-4811-b287-74e417a9@Azure:~$ kc get svc
NAME            TYPE          CLUSTER-IP    EXTERNAL-IP   PORT(S)
AGE
frontend        LoadBalancer  10.0.247.224  <pending>     80:30886/TCP
7m
```

Normally, it would be the reverse, but for demonstration purposes imagine that we are upgrading the frontend version.

5. Change the frontend image line from `image: gcr.io/google-samples/gb-frontend:v4` to the following:

```
image: gcr.io/google-samples/gb-frontend:v3
```

6. Run the following command:

```
kubectl apply -f guestbook-all-in-one.yaml
```

7. You should see the following output:

```
ab443838-9b3e-4811-b287-74e417a9@Azure:~$ kubectl apply -f guestbook-all-
in-one.yaml
service/redis-master unchanged
```

```
deployment.apps/redis-master unchanged
service/redis-slave unchanged
deployment.apps/redis-slave unchanged
service/frontend unchanged
deployment.apps/frontend configured
```

8. Running `kubectl gets events` will show the rolling update strategy that the Deployment uses to update the frontend images:

```
12s          12s          1          frontend.157557b31a134dc7
Deployment                          Normal     ScalingReplicaSet
deployment-controller        Scaled down replica set frontend-56f7975f44 to 2
12s          12s          1          frontend-5785f8455c.157557b31e83d67a
ReplicaSet                          Normal     SuccessfulCreate
replicaset-controller     Created pod: frontend-5785f8455c-z99v2
12s          12s          1          frontend-5785f8455c-
z99v2.157557b31f68ac29        Pod
Normal     Scheduled              default-scheduler     Successfully
assigned default/frontend-5785f8455c-z99v2 to aks-agentpool-18506452-1
12s          12s          1          frontend.157557b31be33765
Deployment                          Normal     ScalingReplicaSet
deployment-controller     Scaled up replica set frontend-5785f8455c to 2
12s          12s          1          frontend-56f7975f44.157557b31bce2beb
ReplicaSet                          Normal     SuccessfulDelete
replicaset-controller     Deleted pod: frontend-56f7975f44-rfd7w
11s          11s          1          frontend-5785f8455c-
z99v2.157557b35b5176f7        Pod          spec.containers{php-redis}
Normal     Pulling                kubelet, aks-agentpool-18506452-1
pulling image "gcr.io/google-samples/gb-frontend:v3"
11s          11s          1          frontend-56f7975f44-
rfd7w.157557b32b25ad47        Pod          spec.containers{php-redis}
Normal     Killing                kubelet, aks-agentpool-18506452-1
Killing container with id docker://php-redis:Need to kill Pod
```

You will also see two replica sets for the frontend, the new one replacing the other one pod at a time:

```
ab443838-9b3e-4811-b287-74e417a9@Azure:~$ kc get rs
NAME                      DESIRED   CURRENT   READY     AGE
frontend-56f7975f44       0         0         0         19m
frontend-5785f8455c       3         3         3         4m
```

9. Finally, let's clean up again by running the `kubectl delete` command:

```
kubectl delete -f guestbook-all-in-one.yaml
```

Congratulations, you have completed the upgrade!

Helm upgrade

This section will explain how to perform upgrades using helm operators in a similar way:

1. Run the following command:

```
helm install stable/wordpress --name handsonaks-wp --set
smtpHost=smtp.google.com --set smtpPort=25 --set smtpPassword=abcd1234 --
set smtpUser=handsonaks@gmail.com --set smtpUsername=handsonaks --set
smtpProtocol=ssl
```

Wait for 5 to 10 minutes for the pods to deploy.

Looking at the tags from `https://hub.docker.com/r/bitnami/wordpress/tags` at the time of writing, we see a new tag of `5.0.2-r9`.

2. Let's live life dangerously and upgrade to the release candidate:

```
helm upgrade handsonaks-wp stable/wordpress --set image.tag=5.0.2-r9
```

When you run the `kubectl get pods` command, you should see two pods for `wordpress`:

```
ab443838-9b3e-4811-b287-74e417a9@Azure:~$ kc describe pods/handsonaks-wp-
wordpress-<new-pod-id> | grep Image
    Image:          docker.io/bitnami/wordpress:5.0.2-r9
    Image ID:       docker-pullable://bitnami
...
ab443838-9b3e-4811-b287-74e417a9@Azure:~$ kc describe pods/handsonaks-wp-
wordpress-<old-pod-id> | grep Image
    Image:          docker.io/bitnami/wordpress:5.0.2
    Image ID:       docker-pullable://bitnami/wordpress@sha256:
```

Running `describe` on them and grepping for images should show that the `wordpress` pod is being redeployed with the `image.tag` set in the second step.

3. Finally, cleaning up the running the following command:

```
helm delete --purge handsonaks-wp
```

Thus, we have upgraded our application using helm operators.

Summary

This was a chapter with tons of information. Our goal was to show how to scale deployments with Kubernetes by not only showing you how to create multiple instances of the software, but also how to debug problems that you might run into.

We started the chapter off by looking at how to define the use of a load balancer and leverage the replica creation feature in Kubernetes to achieve scalability. With this type of scalability, we also achieve failover by using load balancer and multiple instances of the software for stateless applications.

After that, we showed you how to troubleshoot simple problems you might run into, and how to use persistent storage to avoid data loss if a node goes down or needs to be rebooted.

In the next chapter, we will look at how to set up Ingress services and certificate managers to interface with LetsEncrypt.

Single Sign-On with Azure AD **5**

HTTPs has become a necessity for any public-facing website, given phishing attacks. Luckily, with the LetsEncrypt service and helpers in Kubernetes, it is very easy to set verified SSL certificates. In this chapter, we will see how to set up Ingress services and certificate managers to interface with LetsEncrypt.

Different approaches for authentication to the guestbook app will be explored in this chapter. We will look at the `oauth2_proxy` side car for adding authentication to the sample guest app using Azure AD. The reader will be able to secure apps with no built-in authentication easily. The authentication scheme can be extended to use GitHub, Google, GitLab, LinkedIn, or Facebook.

The following topics will be covered in this chapter:

- Authentication and common authentication providers
- Authentication versus authorization (AuthN versus AuthZ)
- Deploying the `oauth2_proxy` side car
- Hints on using GitHub or other authentication providers

Technical requirements

You'll need a modern browser, such as Chrome, Firefox, Safari, or Edge.

You can find the code files for this chapter at `https://github.com/PacktPublishing/Hands-On-Kubernetes-on-Azure`.

HTTPS support

Obtaining **Secure Sockets Layer** (**SSL**) certificates traditionally was an expensive business. If you want to do it cheaply, you could self-sign your certificates, but browsers would complain when opening up your site and identify it as not trusted. The LetsEncrypt service changes all that. You do get some extra benefits with commercial certificate providers, but the certificate issued by LetsEncrypt should be sufficient.

Installing Ingress

Exposing services to the public and routing was "an exercise left to the reader" when Kubernetes started. With the Ingress object, Kubernetes provides a clean way of securely exposing your services. It provides an SSL endpoint and name-based routing. Let's install the nginx version of the Ingress by performing the following steps:

1. Type in the following command to begin the installation:

   ```
   helm install nginx/ingress --set rbac.create=false
   ```

2. Get the exposed IP of the ingress-controller service:

   ```
   kc get svc | grep ingress-controller
   ...-ingress-controller    LoadBalancer   10.0.119.107
   52.175.214.251    80:32533/TCP,443:32382/TCP    2d
   ```

You can browse to the web page by entering `http://<EXTERNAL-IP>` in the browser and it will automatically redirect to the `https://<EXTERNAL-IP>` secure site, where you will get the security warning.

Launching the Guestbook application

To launch the guestbook application, type in the following command:

```
kubectl create -f
https://raw.githubusercontent.com/kubernetes/examples/master/guestbook/all-
in-one/guestbook-all-in-one.yaml
```

Adding Lets Ingress

Use the following `yaml` file to expose the frontend service via the ingress:

```
apiVersion: extensions/v1beta1
kind: Ingress
metadata:
  name: simple-frontend-ingress
  annotations:
    nginx.ingress.kubernetes.io/rewrite-target: /
spec:
  rules:
  - http:
      paths:
      - path: /
        backend:
          serviceName: frontend
          servicePort: 80
```

Use `kubectl apply -f simple-frontend-ingress.yaml` to connect the `nginx-ingress` service to the frontend service. As you can see in the rules section, it tells `nginx` that when someone goes to the path `https://<EXTERNAL-IP>/ use` in the **backend,** the service named frontend is listening on service port `80`.

Go to `https://<EXTERNAL-IP>/` and you should get the following output:

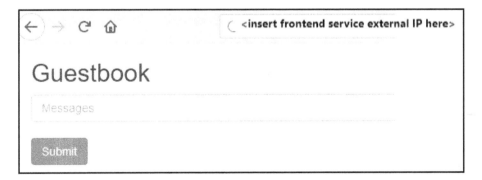

Adding LetsEncrypt

The process of adding LetsEncrypt involves the following steps:

1. Install the certificate manager that interfaces with the LetsEncrypt API to request a certificate for the domain name you specify.

2. Map Azure FQDN to the nginx Ingress public IP.
3. Install the Certificate Issuer that gets the certificate from LetsEncrypt.
4. Create the SSL certificate for a given **Fully-Qualified Domain Name** (**FQDN**).
5. Secure the frontend service section by creating an Ingress to the service with the certificate created in *step 4*.

Installing the certificate manager

The certificate manager (`https://github.com/jetstack/cert-manager`) automates the management and issuance of TLS certificates from various issuing sources. Certificate renewal and ensuring that they are updated periodically is all managed by `cert-manager`, which is a Kubernetes add-on.

The following command installs the cert-manager; at the time of writing, it requires the following workaround to avoid the `custom resource already exists` error:

```
helm install stable/cert-manager \
--name cert-manager \
--set createCustomResource=false \
--set ingressShim.extraArgs='{--default-issuer-name=letsencrypt-prod,--
default-issuer-kind=Issuer}' \
--set rbac.create=false

helm upgrade cert-manager stable/cert-manager \
--set createCustomResource=true \
--set ingressShim.defaultIssuerName=letsencrypt-prod \
--set ingressShim.defaultIssuerKind=ClusterIssuer \
--set rbac.create=false \
--set serviceAccount.create=false
```

Mapping the Azure FQDN to the nginx ingress public IP

LetsEncrypt requires a **publicly-available** DNS entry to verify ownership of the DNS entry *before* it issues the certificate. This ensures that you cannot hijack someone else's site. We have to map the public domain name given to us by azure to the external IP we get from Azure Loadbalancer in order to prove ownership.

Let's map our public domain, say `handsonaks-ingress.westus2.cloudapp.azure.com`, to `<external-ip>` (public IP from "kc get svc |grep ingress").

In case it is already taken, change the FQDN to something more unique to you, such as `handsonaks-yourpetname-ing`.

For LetsEncrypt, we need a valid FQDN in order for the certificate to be issued. LetsEncrypt assumes that if you are able to provide the valid IP for a given **Domain Name System** (**DNS**) entry, you have the rights to the domain. It will issue the certificate **only** after such verification. This is to prevent certificates being issued for your domain by bad actors.

The following script obtains a DNS name for a given Azure Public IP:

```bash
#!/bin/bash
# Public IP address of your ingress controller
IP="<external IP of the ingress service>"

# Name to associate with public IP address
DNSNAME="handsonaks-ingress-<yourname>"
# Get the resource-id of the public ip
PUBLICIPID=$(az network public-ip list --query
"[?ipAddress!=null]|[?contains(ipAddress, '$IP')].[id]" --output tsv)
# Update public ip address with DNS name
az network public-ip update --ids $PUBLICIPID --dns-name $DNSNAME
```

Write down the DNS name. It will be `handsonaks-ingress-<yourname>.westus2.cloudapp.azure.com`.

Installing the certificate issuer

The certificate can be issued by multiple issuers. `letsencrypt-staging`, for example, is for testing purposes. In our case, we are more adventurous, so we will directly use the `letsencrypt-prod` issuer. As usual, use `kubectl apply -f certificate-issuer.yaml`, which has the following contents:

```yaml
apiVersion: certmanager.k8s.io/v1alpha1
kind: ClusterIssuer
metadata:
  name: letsencrypt-prod
spec:
  acme:
    server: https://acme-v02.api.letsencrypt.org/directory
    email: <insert your email here>
    privateKeySecretRef:
      name: letsencrypt-prod
    http01: {}
```

Creating the SSL certificate

We're almost there; let's request a certificate from the `letsencrypt` service:

```
apiVersion: certmanager.k8s.io/v1alpha1
kind: Certificate
metadata:
  name: tls-secret
spec:
  secretName: tls-secret
  dnsNames:
  - handsonaks-ingress-<yourname>.westus2.cloudapp.azure.com
  acme:
    config:
    - http01:
        ingressClass: nginx
      domains:
      - handsonaks-ingress-<yourname>.westus2.cloudapp.azure.com
  issuerRef:
    name: letsencrypt-prod
    kind: ClusterIssuer
```

The certificate manager obtains the certificate for the domain specified and handles the handshake required for verification. Pretty cool stuff.

Securing the frontend service connection

Let's create the lets-encrypt HTTPs frontend tunnel. Following is the Quick status update:

- Certificate manager for interfacing with the `letsencrypt` service √
- Public DNS name for our ingress √
- Certificate for our public FQDN

The missing piece is the connection between our public ingress to the frontend service. The following code will create that for you:

```
 1 apiVersion: extensions/v1beta1
 2 kind: Ingress
 3 metadata:
 4   name: frontend-aks-ingress
 5   annotations:
 6     kubernetes.io/ingress.class: nginx
 7     certmanager.k8s.io/cluster-issuer: letsencrypt-prod
 8     nginx.ingress.kubernetes.io/rewrite-target: /
 9 spec:
10   tls:
```

```
11    - hosts:
12      - handsonaks-ingress.westus2.cloudapp.azure.com
13      secretName: tls-secret
14    rules:
15    - host: handsonaks-ingress.westus2.cloudapp.azure.com
16      http:
17        paths:
18        - path: /
19          backend:
20            serviceName: frontend
21            servicePort: 80
```

Let's break down the preceding code:

- **Lines 1-2**: Specifies that we want the Ingress resource.
- **Lines 3-8**: Gives it a name (`frontend-aks-ingress`) and, uses the `nginx` ingress, backed by the `letsencrypt-prod` certificate issuer, along with `nginx` specific rewrite target rule, to make the browser think that `nginx` is the root for all `html/css/js` files.
- **Lines 9-13**: Tells `nginx` ingress to obtain the certificates from `secret tls-secret`, which is set by the cert manager once it gets it for the `handsonaks-ingress.westus2.cloudapp.azure.com` host from the LetsEncrypt service.
- **Lines 14-21**: Specifies to nginx that any request that is coming for `handsonaks-ingress.westus2.cloudapp.azure.com` on the / path is handled by the `frontend` service on port `80`.

You can verify that the service is up by launching `https://handsonaks-ingress.westus2.cloudapp.azure.com/`. You should see the following:

Authentication versus authorization

Authentication (AuthN) is very often mixed up with authorization (AuthZ). It generally takes multiple attempts to understand the difference and we *still* get confused. The source of confusion is that most people think the authentication provider and the authorization provider are the *same*. In our WordPress example, WordPress provides the authentication (has the username and password) *and* authorization (stores the users under admin or user roles, for example). The implementation in the code (at least initially) would be mixing up authentication and authorization also (*if (admin) do this; else do that*). Even the names can be confusing. OAuth is an authorization protocol, whereas we are using the `oauth2_proxy` for authentication.

Authentication deals with identity (who are you?), and in general requires a trusted provider (such as Google, GitHub, or Azure).

Authorization deals with permissions (what are you trying to do?), and is very implementation specific in terms of what application resources needs to be protected.

We are going to use Azure AD for authentication to our guestbook service.

Authentication and common authN providers

Our guestbook application is open to all and lets anyone with the public IP access the service. The image by itself has no authentication support and we cannot request the code authors to add authentication just for us. A common problem is wanting to apply policy separately from implementation. The common approach used for this purpose is the sidecar pattern (`https://docs.microsoft.com/en-us/azure/architecture/patterns/sidecar`). It is similar to aspect-oriented programming.

Authentication deals with verifying whether you are who you say you are. The normal verification system is via username and password. The assumption is that *only you* know your username and password and therefore you are the person who is logging in. Obviously, with recent hacks, it has not proven to be sufficient, hence the implementation of two-factor authentication and multi-factor authentication. On top of that, it has become very hard for people to remember their multiple user accounts and passwords. To help alleviate that, authentication is provided as a service by multiple providers with support for OAuth or SAML. Here are some of the well-known providers:

- Google (`https://github.com/pusher/oauth2_proxy#google-auth-provider`)
- Azure (`https://github.com/pusher/oauth2_proxy#azure-auth-provider`)

- Facebook (https://github.com/pusher/oauth2_proxy#facebook-auth-provider)
- GitHub (https://github.com/pusher/oauth2_proxy#github-auth-provider)
- GitLab (https://github.com/pusher/oauth2_proxy#gitlab-auth-provider)
- LinkedIn (https://github.com/pusher/oauth2_proxy#linkedin-auth-provider

In the following sections, we will use a sidecar implementation, oauth2_proxy, to implement authentication for our guestbook example.

Deploying the oauth2_proxy side car

We are going to implement oauth2_proxy from bitly (https://github.com/bitly/oauth2_proxy). We will be following the steps indicated in the documentation for Azure AD (https://docs.microsoft.com/en-us/azure/active-directory/).

First, register an app with Azure AD as shown in the following screenshot:

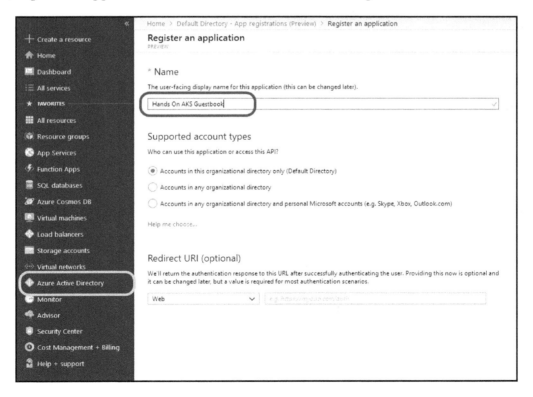

Next, create a client ID secret by performing the following steps:

1. Select **Certificates & secrets** and go to **New client secret**:

2. Add the secret:

3. Click on the Copy icon and save the secret in a safe place:

DESCRIPTION	EXPIRES	VALUE
Guestbook secret	12/31/2019	wu:q{%.}+^&X(K;_!K|0:1+k(v^.E%^]%w)7;);*NL9$;>!!(

4. Save the client and the tenant ID:

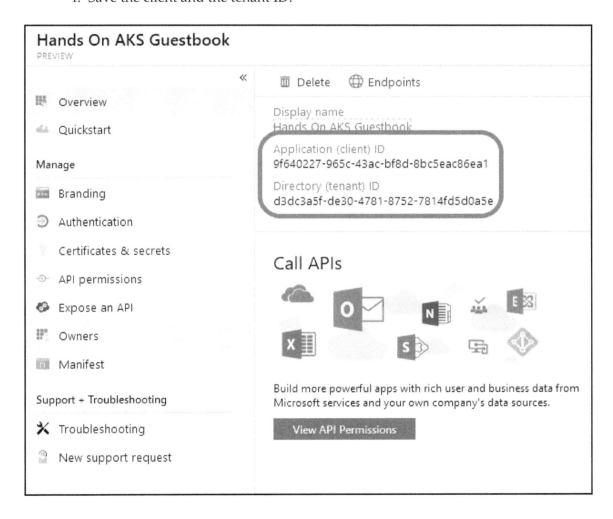

After creating the client ID secret, we will now launch `oauth2_proxy` with the following YAML file:

```yaml
apiVersion: extensions/v1beta1
kind: Deployment
metadata:
  name: oauth2-proxy
  namespace: kube-system
spec:
  replicas: 1
  selector:
    matchLabels:
      app: oauth2-proxy
  template:
    metadata:
      labels:
        app: oauth2-proxy
    spec:
      containers:
      - args:
        - --provider=azure
        - --email-domain=microsoft.com
        - --upstream=http://10.0.83.95:80
        - --http-address=0.0.0.0:4180
        - --azure-tenant=d3dc3a5f-de30-4781-8752-7814fd5d0a5e
        env:
          - name: OAUTH2_PROXY_CLIENT_ID
            value: 9f640227-965c-43ac-bf8d-8bc5eac86ea1
          - name: OAUTH2_PROXY_CLIENT_SECRET
            value: "wu:q{%.}+^&X(K;_!K|0:1+k(v^.E%^]%w)7;);*NL9$;>!l()_"
          - name: OAUTH2_PROXY_COOKIE_SECRET
            value: 9ju360pxM2nVQdQqQZ4Dtg==
        image: docker.io/colemickens/oauth2_proxy:latest
        imagePullPolicy: Always
        name: oauth2-proxy
        ports:
        - containerPort: 4180
          protocol: TCP
```

Next, Oauth2 needs to be exposed as a service so that the ingress can talk to it by running the following code:

```yaml
apiVersion: v1
kind: Service
metadata:
  name: oauth2-proxy
  namespace: default
spec:
```

```
ports:
- name: http
  port: 4180
  protocol: TCP
  targetPort: 4180
selector:
  app: oauth2-proxy
```

Create an ingress so that any URL link that goes to `handsonaks-ingress-<yourname>.westus2.cloudapp.azure.com/oauth` will be redirected to the `oauth2-proxy` service.

The same `letsencrypt` certificate is used here:

```
apiVersion: extensions/v1beta1
kind: Ingress
metadata:
  name: oauth2-proxy-ingress
  annotations:
    kubernetes.io/ingress.class: nginx
    kubernetes.io/tls-acme: "true"
spec:
  tls:
  - hosts:
    - handsonaks-ingress.westus2.cloudapp.azure.com
    secretName: tls-secret
  rules:
  - host: handsonaks-ingress.westus2.cloudapp.azure.com
    http:
      paths:
      - path: /oauth2
        backend:
          serviceName: oauth2-proxy
          servicePort: 4180
```

Finally, we will link the `oauth2` proxy to the frontend service by creating an ingress that configures `nginx` so that authentication is checked using the paths in `auth-url` and `auth-signin`. If it is successful, the traffic is redirected to the backend service (in our case it is the frontend service).

The following code performs the redirection once authentication is successful:

```
apiVersion: extensions/v1beta1
kind: Ingress
metadata:
  name: frontend-oauth2-ingress
  annotations:
    kubernetes.io/ingress.class: nginx
    nginx.ingress.kubernetes.io/auth-url:
```

```
  "http://oauth2-proxy.default.svc.cluster.local:4180/oauth2/auth"
      nginx.ingress.kubernetes.io/auth-signin:
  "http://handsonaks-ingress-<yourname>.westus2.cloudapp.azure.com/oauth2/sta
  rt"
      nginx.ingress.kubernetes.io/ssl-redirect: "false"
      nginx.ingress.kubernetes.io/rewrite-target: /
spec:
  rules:
  - host: handsonaks-ingress-<yourname>.westus2.cloudapp.azure.com
    http:
      paths:
      - path: /
        backend:
          serviceName: frontend
          servicePort: 80
```

We are done with configuration. You can now log in with your existing Microsoft account to the service at `https://handsonaks-ingress-<yourname>.westus2.cloudapp.azure.net/`.

 `oauth2-proxy` supports multiple authentication providers, such as GitHub and Google. Only the `oauth2-proxy` deployment's `yaml` has to be changed with the right service to change the `auth` provider. Please see the section at `https://github.com/pusher/oauth2_proxy#oauth-provider-configuration`.

Summary

In this chapter, we added access control to our guestbook application without actually changing the source code of it by using the sidecar pattern in Kubernetes (`https://kubernetes.io/blog/2015/06/the-distributed-system-toolkit-patterns/`). We started by getting the Kubernetes ingress objects to redirect to a `https://....` secured site. Then we installed the certificate manager that interfaces with the LetsEncrypt API to request a certificate for the domain name you specified in the next steps. We leveraged a Certificate Issuer, which gets the certificate from LetsEncrypt, and created the actual certificate for a given **Fully-Qualified Domain Name (FQDN)**. We then created an Ingress to the service with the certificate we'd created. Finally, we jumped into authentication (AuthN) and authorization (AuthZ), and showed you how to leverage AzureAD as an authentication provider for the guestbook application.

You learned how to secure your applications on an enterprise scale. By integrating with Azure Active Directory, you can enable any application to link to an organization's Active Directory. This alone is worth more than the price of this book.

In the next chapter, you will learn how to be a superhero, by predicting and fixing issues before they occur through proactive monitoring and alerts. You will also learn to use your X-ray vision to quickly identify root causes when errors do occur, and learn how to debug applications running on AKS. You will be able to perform the right fixes once you have identified the root cause.

6
Monitoring the AKS Cluster and the Application

In this chapter, you will learn how to monitor your cluster and the applications running on it. We will also show the use of the **Microsoft Operations Management Suite (OMS)** agent and the integration with Azure Portal, as well as set up alerts for critical events on the AKS cluster. You will be proactive in monitoring your cluster and the applications running on it, and you will be a hero for being able to proactively prevent errors from happening (launching more nodes when the cluster is CPU-constrained, for example) and for quickly resolving issues when they do happen.

In brief, the following topics will be covered in this chapter:

- The `kubectl` commands for monitoring applications
- Debugging applications
- Review metrics reported by Kubernetes
- Review metrics from OMS

Technical requirements

You will require a modern browser such as Chrome, Firefox, Safari, or Edge.

You will find the code files for this chapter by accessing the following link: `https://github.com/PacktPublishing/Hands-On-Kubernetes-on-Azure`.

Commands for monitoring applications

Monitoring deployed applications on AKS along with monitoring Kubernetes health is essential to provide reliable service to your customers. There are two primary use cases for monitoring:

- Debugging applications (used mostly when deploying/upgrading apps)
- On-going monitoring to get alerts if something is not behaving as expected

We will handle the first use case of debugging when deploying/upgrading applications. The same methodology also applies for debugging running applications for which the commands are as follows:

```
kubectl get xxx
kubectl logs xxx
```

Before we start, we are going to have a clean start with our guestbook example.

If you have guestbook already running in your cluster, delete it by running the following command on the Azure Cloud Shell:

```
kubectl delete -f guestbook-all-in-one.yaml
```

Recreate the guestbook again using the following command:

```
kubectl create -f guestbook-all-in-one.yaml
```

While the `create` command is running, we will watch the progress in the following sections.

kubectl get command

To see the overall picture of deployed applications, x provides the `get` command. The `get` command lists the resources that you specify. Resources can be pods, replication controllers, ingress, nodes, deployments, secrets, and so on. We have already run this in the previous chapters to verify whether our application is ready to be used or not. Perform the following steps:

1. Run the following `get` command, which will get us the resources and their statuses:

```
kubectl get all
```

You will get something like this, as shown in the following block:

```
NAME                                                        READY
STATUS     RESTARTS    AGE
pod/frontend-5785f8455c-2dsgt                               0/1
Pending    0           9s
pod/frontend-5785f8455c-f8knz                               0/1
Pending    0           9s
pod/frontend-5785f8455c-p9mh9                               0/1
Pending    0           9s
pod/redis-master-6b464554c8-sghfh                           0/1
Pending    0           9s
pod/redis-slave-b58dc4644-2ngwx                             0/1
Pending    0           9s
pod/redis-slave-b58dc4644-581v2                             0/1
Pending    0           9s
```

. . .

2. Now to view the pods, run the following command:

`kubectl get -w pods`

The command doesn't exit and changes output *only* if the state of any pod changes. For example, you will see an output that is similar to this:

```
ab443838-9b3e-4811-b287-74e417a9@Azure:~$ kubectl get -w pods
NAME                                                        READY
STATUS     RESTARTS    AGE
frontend-5785f8455c-2dsgt                                   0/1
Pending    0           5m
frontend-5785f8455c-f8knz                                   0/1
Pending    0           5m
frontend-5785f8455c-p9mh9                                   0/1
Pending    0           5m
redis-master-6b464554c8-sghfh                               0/1
Pending    0           5m
redis-slave-b58dc4644-2ngwx                                 0/1
Pending    0           5m
redis-slave-b58dc4644-581v2                                 0/1
Pending    0           5m
```

If you wait long enough, you will get the following:

```
frontend-5785f8455c-f8knz        0/1     ContainerCreating    0          8m
frontend-5785f8455c-2dsgt        0/1     ContainerCreating    0          8m
redis-master-6b464554c8-sghfh    0/1       ContainerCreating    0            8m
redis-slave-b58dc4644-581v2      0/1     ContainerCreating    0          8m
```

```
redis-slave-b58dc4644-2ngwx     0/1        ContainerCreating    0            8m
frontend-5785f8455c-p9mh9      0/1        ContainerCreating    0            8m
frontend-5785f8455c-f8knz      1/1        Running    0           8m
frontend-5785f8455c-2dsgt      1/1        Running    0           8m
redis-master-6b464554c8-sghfh     1/1        Running    0            8m
redis-slave-b58dc4644-581v2     1/1        Running    0           8m
redis-slave-b58dc4644-2ngwx     1/1        Running    0           8m
frontend-5785f8455c-p9mh9      1/1        Running    0           8m
```

You will see *only* the pods are shown. Also, you get a view of the state changes of the pods that kubernetes handles. The first column is the pod name (`frontend-5785f8455c-f8knz`), for example. The second column is how many containers in the pod are ready over the total number of containers in the pod (`0/1` initially meaning 0 containers are up while a total of `1` is expected). The third column is the status (`Pending/ContainerCreating/Running/...`). The fourth column is the number of restarts. The fifth column is the age (when the pod was asked to be created).

Press *Ctrl + C* to stop the monitoring.

Once the state changes, you don't see the history of state changes. For example, if you run the same command now, it will be stuck at the running state till you press *Ctrl + C*:

```
ab443838-9b3e-4811-b287-74e417a9@Azure:~$ kubectl get -w pods
NAME                                                          READY
STATUS     RESTARTS     AGE
frontend-5785f8455c-2dsgt                                     1/1
Running    0           26m
frontend-5785f8455c-f8knz                                     1/1
Running    0           26m
frontend-5785f8455c-p9mh9                                     1/1
Running    0           26m
redis-master-6b464554c8-sghfh                                 1/1
Running    0           26m
redis-slave-b58dc4644-2ngwx                                   1/1
Running    0           26m
redis-slave-b58dc4644-581v2                                   1/1
Running    0           26m
```

To see the history if something goes wrong, run the following command:

```
kubectl get events
```

Kubernetes maintains events for only one hour by default. All the commands work only if the event was fired within the past hour.

If everything went well, you should have an output something similar to the following one:

```
    42s           42s              1              frontend-5785f8455c-
wxsdm.1581ea340ab4ab56         Pod
Normal    Scheduled                   default-scheduler
Successfully assigned default/frontend-5785f8455c-wxsdm to aks-
agentpool-26533852-0
42s           42s              1              frontend-5785f8455c.1581ea34098640c9
ReplicaSet                              Normal    SuccessfulCreate
replicaset-controller                Created pod: frontend-5785f8455c-1kjgc
40s           40s              1
frontend-5785f8455c-2trpg.1581ea3487c328b5         Pod
spec.containers{php-redis}    Normal    Pulled                kubelet, aks-
agentpool-26533852-0    Container image "gcr.io/google-samples/gb-
frontend:v3" already present on machine
40s           40s              1
frontend-5785f8455c-2trpg.1581ea34b5abca9e         Pod
spec.containers{php-redis}    Normal    Created               kubelet, aks-
agentpool-26533852-0    Created container
39s           39s              1
frontend-5785f8455c-2trpg.1581ea34d18c96f8         Pod
spec.containers{php-redis}    Normal    Started               kubelet, aks-
agentpool-26533852-0    Started container
```

The general states for a pod are `Scheduled->Pulled->Created->Started`. As we will see next, things can fail at any of the states, and we need to use the `kubectl get` command to dig deeper.

kubectl describe command

The `kubectl` events command lists all the events for the entire namespace. If you are interested in just a pod, you can use the following command:

```
kubectl describe pods
```

The preceding command lists all the information about all pods.

If you want information on a particular pod, you can type the following:

```
kubeclt describe pod/<pod-name>
```

You will get an output similar to the one here:

```
Name:                  frontend-5785f8455c-2trpg
Namespace:             default
...
Node:                  aks-agentpool-26533852-0/10.240.0.4
Start Time:            Sun, 10 Feb 2019 05:40:55 +0000
Labels:                app=guestbook
                       pod-template-hash=1341940117
                       tier=frontend
Annotations:           <none>
Status:                Running
IP:                    10.244.0.87
Controlled By:         ReplicaSet/frontend-5785f8455c
Containers:
  php-redis:
...
    Image:             gcr.io/google-samples/gb-frontend:v3
    ...
    Port:              80/TCP
    Host Port:         0/TCP
...
    Environment:
      GET_HOSTS_FROM:                    dns
Events:
  Type    Reason     Age    From                      Message
  ----    ------     ----   ----                      -------
  Normal  Scheduled  26m    default-scheduler         Successfully
assigned default/frontend-5785f8455c-2trpg to aks-agentpool-26533852-0
  Normal  Pulled     26m    kubelet, aks-agentpool-26533852-0  Container
image "gcr.io/google-samples/gb-frontend:v3" already present on machine
  Normal  Created    26m    kubelet, aks-agentpool-26533852-0  Created
container
  Normal  Started    26m    kubelet, aks-agentpool-26533852-0  Started
container
```

From the description, you can get the node on which the pod is running, how long it was running, its internal IP address, `docker` image name, ports exposed, `env` variables, and the events (within the past hour).

In the preceding example, the pod name is `frontend-5785f8455c-2trpg`. Note that it has the `<replicaset name>-<random 5 chars>` format. The `replicaset` name itself is randomly generated from the deployment name `frontend`.

The namespace under which the pod runs is default. So far we have been just using the default namespace, appropriately named default. In the next chapters, we will see how namespaces help us to isolate pods.

The next section that is important from the preceding output is the *node* section.

```
Node: aks-agentpool-26533852-0/10.240.0.4
```

The node section lets us know which physical node/VM that the pod is actually running on. If the pod is repeatedly starting or having issues running and everything else seems OK, there might be an issue with the node. Having this information is essential to perform advanced debugging.

The following is the time the pod was initially scheduled:

```
Start Time: Sun, 10 Feb 2019 05:40:55 +0000
```

It doesn't mean that the pod has been running from that time. So, the time can be misleading in that sense. The actual uptime of the pod would be dependent on whether it was moved from a node to another, or the node it was on went down.

Connections between resources are made using `Labels` as shown here:

```
Labels:           app=guestbook
                  pod-template-hash=1341940117
                  tier=frontend
```

This is how connections such as `Service->Deployment->ReplicaSet->Pod` are made. If you see that traffic is not being routed to a pod from a service, this is the first thing you should check. If the labels don't match, the resources won't attach.

The following shows the internal IP of the pod and its status:

```
Status:           Running
IP:               10.244.0.87
```

When a service directs its traffic or another container wants to talk to the containers in this pod, this is the IP that they will see. This IP is very useful when resolving application issues. Let's say you want to know why the frontend is not able to reach the server, you could find the server pod IP and try pinging it from the frontend container.

The containers running in the pod and the ports that are exposed are listed in the following block:

```
Containers:
  php-redis:
  . . .
    Image:        gcr.io/google-samples/gb-frontend:v3
    . . .
    Port:         80/TCP
    Host Port:    0/TCP
```

```
...
    Environment:
        GET_HOSTS_FROM:                    dns
```

In this case, we are getting the `gb-frontend` container with the `v3` tag from the `gcr.io` container registry, and the repository name is `google-samples`.

Port 80 is exposed for outside traffic. Since each pod has its own IP, the same port can be exposed for multiple containers of the same pod running even on the same host. This is a huge management advantage as we don't have to worry about port collisions. The port that needs to be configured is also fixed so that scripts can be written simply without the logic of figuring out which port actually got allocated for the pod.

Any events that occurred in the previous hour show up here:

```
Events:
```

Debugging applications

Now that we have a basic understanding of how to monitor deployments, we can start seeing how we can debug issues with deployments.

In this section, we will introduce common errors and determine how to debug and fix them.

If not done already, run the following command:

```
kubectl create -f guestbook-all-in-one.yaml
```

After sometime, the services should be up and running.

Image Pull errors

In this section, we are going to introduce image pull errors by setting the image tag value to a non-existent one.

Run the following command on Azure Cloud Shell:

```
kubectl edit deployment/frontend
```

Next, change the image tag from `v3` to `v_non_existent` by running the following commands:

```
image: gcr.io/google-samples/gb-frontend:v3
image: gcr.io/google-samples/gb-frontend:v_non_existent
```

Now save it.

Running the following command lists all the pods in the current namespace:

```
kc get pods
```

The preceding command should show errors as shown here:

```
pod/frontend-5489947457-hvtq2 0/1  ErrImagePull   0          4s
```

Run the following command to get all the errors:

```
kubectl describe pods/frontend-5489947457-<random chars>
```

A sample error output that should be similar to your output is shown here. The key error line is highlighted in bold:

```
Events:
  Type       Reason     Age             From
Message
  ----       ------     ----            ----
------
  Normal     Scheduled  2m                      default-scheduler
Successfully assigned default/frontend-5489947457-hvtq2 to aks-
agentpool-26533852-0
  Normal     Pulling    1m (x4 over 2m)  kubelet, aks-agentpool-26533852-0
pulling image "gcr.io/google-samples/gb-frontend:v_non_existent"
  Warning    Failed     1m (x4 over 2m)  kubelet, aks-agentpool-26533852-0
Failed to pull image "gcr.io/google-samples/gb-frontend:v_non_existent":
rpc error: code = Unknown desc = Error response from daemon: manifest for
gcr.io/google-samples/gb-frontend:v_non_existent not found
  Warning    Failed     1m (x4 over 2m)  kubelet, aks-agentpool-26533852-0
Error: ErrImagePull
  Normal     BackOff    1m (x6 over 2m)  kubelet, aks-agentpool-26533852-0
Back-off pulling image "gcr.io/google-samples/gb-frontend:v_non_existent"
  Warning    Failed     1m (x7 over 2m)  kubelet, aks-agentpool-26533852-0
Error: ImagePullBackOff
```

So, the events clearly show that the image does not exist. Errors such as passing invalid credentials to private Docker repositories will also show up here.

Let's fix the error, by setting the image tag back to `v3`:

```
kubectl edit deployment/frontend
image: gcr.io/google-samples/gb-frontend:v_non_existent
image: gcr.io/google-samples/gb-frontend:v3
```

Save the file, and the deployment should get automatically fixed. You can verify it by getting the events for the pods again.

 Because we did a rolling update, the frontend was continuously available with zero downtime. Kubernetes recognized a problem with the new specification and stopped rolling out the changes automatically.

Application errors

We will see how to debug an application error. The errors in this section will be self-induced similar to the last section. The method of debugging the issue is the same as the one we have used to debug errors on running applications.

 Most errors come from `mis-configuration`, where it can be fixed by editing the specification. Errors in the application code itself requires a new image to be built and used.

Scaling down the frontend

With `replicas=3`, the request can be handled by any of the pods. To introduce the application `error` and note the errors, we need to make changes in all three of them. Let's make our life easier, by scaling the replicas to `1`, so that we can make changes in one pod only:

```
kubectl scale --replicas=1 deployment/frontend
```

Introducing an app "error"

In this case, we are going to make the `Submit` button fail to work.

We need to modify the application code for that.

To properly do this, you need to create a new image with the wrong code, upload it to your Docker repository and use that image for serving the application.

We will use the `kubectl exec` command that lets you run the commands on a pod. With the `-it` option, it attaches an interactive terminal to the pod and gives us a shell that we can run our commands on. The following command launches a Bash Terminal on the pod:

```
kubectl exec -it <frontend-pod-name> bash
```

Once you are in the container shell, run the following:

```
apt update
apt install -y vim
```

The preceding code installs the vim editor so that we can edit the file to introduce `error`.

You can run another instance of the cloud shell by clicking the button shown. This will allow debugging while editing the application code:

In shell #1, open the `guestbook.php` file:

```
vim guestbook.php
```

Add the following line after the `#18` line:

```
$host = 'localhost';
```

The file will look similar to the following:

```
18    if ($_GET['cmd'] == 'set') {
19        $host = 'localhost';
20        $client = new Predis\Client([
```

We are introducing an error where reading messages would work, but not writing them. We do this by asking the frontend to connect to the Redis master at the non-existent local host server. The writes should fail.

Open up your guestbook and note the entries there:

Now add a new entry and click on **Submit**:

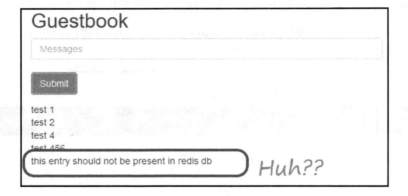

This shows that the app is not production ready. If we did not know any better, we would have thought the entry was written safely. So what is going on?

Without going too much into the application design, the way the app works is as follows:

- It grabs all the entries on startup and stores them in its cache
- Any time a new entry is added, the object is added to its cache **independent** of whether the server acknowledges that it was written.

If you have network debugging tools turned on your browser, you can catch the response from the server.

To verify that it has not been written to the database, hit the Refresh button in your browser; you will see only the initial entries and the new entry has disappeared:

As an app developer or operator, you probably get a ticket like this: *After the new deployment, new entries are not persisted. Fix it.*

Logs

The first step is to get the logs. On the second shell, run the following:

```
kubectl logs <frontend-pod-name>
```

You will see entries, like this:

```
"GET
/guestbook.php?cmd=set&key=messages&value=,test%201,test%202,test%204,test%
20456,this%20entry%20should%20not%20be%20present%20in%20redis%20db
HTTP/1.1" 200 1345 "https://handsonaks-ingress.westus2.cloudapp.azure.com/"
"Mozilla/5.0 (Windows NT 10.0; Win64; x64; rv:65.0) Gecko/20100101
Firefox/65.0"
```

So you know that the error is somewhere when writing to the database in the "set" section of the code.

On the other cloud shell window, edit the file to print out debug messages:

```
if ($_GET['cmd'] == 'set') {
    if(!defined('STDOUT')) define('STDOUT', fopen('php://stdout', 'w'));
    fwrite(STDOUT, "hostname at the beginning of 'set' command ");
    fwrite(STDOUT, $host);
    fwrite(STDOUT, "\n");
```

Add a new entry to the browser and look at the logs again:

```
kc logs <frontend-pod-name>
```

You will see this entry:

```
hostname at the beginning of 'set' command redis-master
```

So we "know" that the error is between this line and the starting of the client, so the setting of the `$host = 'localhost'` must be the offending error. This error is not as uncommon as you think it would be, and as we just saw could have easily gone through QA unless there had been a specific instruction to refresh the browser. It could have worked perfectly will for the developer, as they could have a running `redis` server on the local machine.

Delete the offending line, and save the file:

```
18   if ($_GET['cmd'] == 'set') {
19      if(!defined('STDOUT')) define('STDOUT', fopen('php://stdout',
'w'));
20      fwrite(STDOUT, "hostname at the beginning of 'set' command");
21      fwrite(STDOUT, $host);
22      fwrite(STDOUT, "\n");
23      $client = new Predis\Client([
```

Add a new entry to the browser and hit Refresh to be sure:

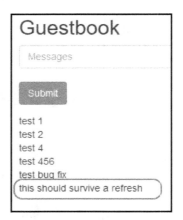

Check the browser network logs to be sure that the `redis` backend database is being hit and the entries are retrieved.

The following points summarize some common errors and methods to fix the errors:

- Errors can come in many shapes and forms.
- Most of the errors encountered by the deployment team are configuration issues.
- Logs are your friend.
- Adding `kubectl exec` to a container is your next best friend.
- **Note this a serious security risk, as it pretty much lets the operator do what they want**.
- Anything printed to `stdout` and `stderr` shows up in the logs (independent of the application/language/logging framework).

Metrics reported by Kubernetes

Kubernetes has a dashboard add-on, which is really cool and shows many metrics in a consumable form. However, it is a serious security risk and requires complicated configuration to set up securely.

We won't be installing it, as you get the same benefit, without the hassle from Azure Kubernetes Monitoring itself. If you still want to do it, please see `https://blog.heptio. com/on-securing-the-kubernetes-dashboard-16b09b1b7aca`.

We are going to list the metrics available by `kubectl`.

Node status and consumption

Run the following command to get information about the nodes on the cluster:

`kubectl get nodes`

The following lists their name, status, and age:

```
NAME                        STATUS    ROLES    AGE    VERSION
aks-agentpool-26533852-0    Ready     agent    34d    v1.11.5
```

You can get more information by passing the `-o wide` option:

```
kubectl get -o wide nodes
```

The output lists, the underlying `OS-IMAGE`, internal IP, and other useful information can be obtained with the following:

```
NAME STATUS ROLES AGE VERSION INTERNAL-IP EXTERNAL-IP OS-IMAGE KERNEL-
VERSION CONTAINER-RUNTIME
aks-agentpool-26533852-0 Ready agent 34d v1.11.5 10.240.0.4 <none> Ubuntu
16.04.5 LTS    4.15.0-1036-azure   docker://3.0.1
```

You can find out which nodes are consuming the most resources, using the following:

```
kubectl top nodes
```

It shows the CPU and memory usage of the nodes:

```
NAME                       CPU(cores)    CPU%      MEMORY(bytes)    MEMORY%
aks-agentpool-26533852-0   146m          7%        1233Mi           23%
```

The same set of commands can be run for pods.

Metrics reported from OMS

Azure Portal shows many of the metrics that you would like to see combined with authorization as only personnel with access to the portal can see these metrics.

AKS Insights

The **Insights** section of the AKS tab provides most of the metrics you need to know about your cluster. It also has the ability to drill down to the container level. You can also see the logs of the container.

 Logs of a container could contain sensitive information. So the rights to review logs should be controlled and audited.

Cluster metrics

Insights show the cluster metrics. The following screenshot shows the CPU utilization and the memory utilization of all the nodes in the cluster:

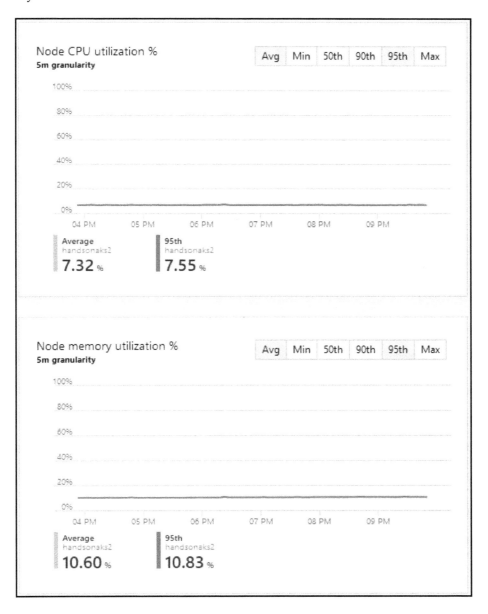

Scrolling down shows the node and pod status monitoring. This is important if you have nodes going from the **Ready** to **Not Ready** state. This would be very useful information when contacting Azure support if something goes wrong. Similarly, if pods are in a failed state, you can find that out here:

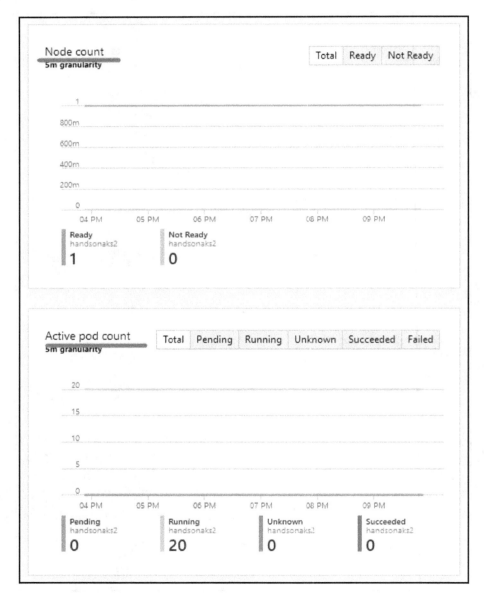

Container metrics, logs, and environmental variables

Clicking on the container tab lists the container metrics, environment variables, and access to its logs as shown in the following screenshot:

 ENV variables can contain sensitive information, so access to insights should be tightly controlled through RBAC.

Apart from the logs, it also shows the environment variables that are set for the container:

Logs

Log filtering helps in obtaining the `kube` events of interest that happened before the default window of an hour.

Filtering by container name can also be done, without resorting to the Azure cloud shell.

The following screenshot shows the log information, such as the event time, node, resource type or object kind, namespace, resource name, and message. The pod with the `ImagePullBackOff` error is highlighted as follows:

Summary

We started the chapter by showing how to use the `kubectl` events to monitor the application. Then we showed how powerful the created logs are to debug the application. The logs contain all the information that is written to `stdout` and `stderr`. We also touched on the Kuberenetes dashboards and showed you how to use the Kubernetes metrics for the operational monitoring of your deployments. Lastly, we explained the use of OMS to show the AKS metrics and environment variables, as well as logs with log filtering. You now have the skills to set alerts on any metric that you would like to be notified of by leveraging Azure Insights. You also learned how to debug application and cluster issues through the use of `kubectl` and OMS monitoring.

In the next chapter, we will learn how to secure an AKS cluster with role-based security, leveraging Azure Active Directory as an authentication provider.

Operation and Maintenance of AKS Applications

7

In production systems, you need to allow different personnel access to certain resources; this is known as **role-based access control** (**RBAC**). This chapter will take you through how you can turn on RBAC on AKS and practice assigning different roles with different rights. Users would be able to verify that their access is denied when trying to modify resources that they do not have access to. The benefits of establishing RBAC are that it acts not only as a guardrail against the accidental deletion of critical resources but also an important security feature to limit full access to the cluster to roles that really need it.

The following topics will be covered in this chapter:

- Service roles in Kubernetes
- Attaching service roles to Azure AD users
- Verifying RBAC

Technical requirements

You will need a modern web browser, such as Chrome, Firefox, or Edge.

Service roles in Kubernetes

Using the cloud shell, we have been acting as *root*, which allowed us to pretty much do anything and everything in the cluster. For production use cases, this root access is dangerous and not allowed in selected regulated environments. It is a generally-accepted best practice to use the **principle of least privilege** (**PoLP**) to log into any computer system, so as to avoid unintentional downtime through deleting key resources while thinking that you were operating on the local cluster (been there, done that). Anywhere between 22% and 29% (`https://blog.storagecraft.com/data-loss-statistics-infographic/`) of data loss is attributed to human error. You don't want to be part of that statistic (it is very painful).

Kubernetes developers realized this was a problem, and added RBAC along with the concept of service roles to control access to the cluster.

Service roles let you assign read-only and read/write access to Kubernetes resources. You can say person X has read-only access to the pods running in a namespace. The neat thing about AKS is that the person can be tied to Azure Active Directory (which in turn can be linked to your corporate Active Directory via an SSO solution).

Deleting any AKS cluster without RBAC

If you have a cluster already running, to save costs and reduce variability, it is recommended that you delete the cluster before starting. As with the preceding warning, it is assumed that you are following this book using your own personal account. Be very careful before deleting the cluster if you are using your corporate or shared account.

The following screenshot shows how to delete a cluster on Azure Portal:

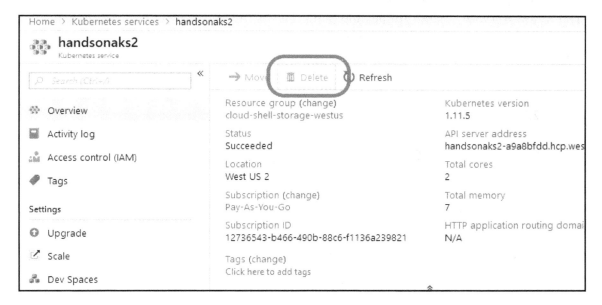

Creating an AKS cluster with the Azure AD RBAC support

Azure Active Directory (**AAD**) provides a hosted Active Directory that is a scalable and convenient way to manage users for any application. The ability to easily link an AAD with your organization's **Single-Sign-On** (**SSO**) provider is a tremendous benefit. Since most organizations have Office 365 online, by default they have an Azure AD instance. As an operator, by linking the Azure AD to Kubernetes RBAC, you don't have to worry about off-boarding people and, as an app owner, you can easily assign members to Azure AD groups.

To start, we need to create Azure AD applications to link to our Kubernetes cluster. The steps we are going to follow are pretty much verbatim from `https://docs.microsoft.com/en-us/azure/aks/aad-integration`.

Creating the Azure AD server application

The Azure AD server is the application that is used to get the users in the default Azure AD directory associated with your account. To create the application, perform the following steps:

1. Select the Azure **Active Directory -> App registrations ->New application** registration.
2. Enter the details as shown here:

3. Click on **Create** and then click on **Manifest** to edit it:

4. Change `groupMembershipClaims` from null to `All`:

```
 1  {
 2      "appId": "c25f7ab8-7217-4b2e-90d9-aac99718a4df",
 3      "appRoles": [],
 4      "availableToOtherTenants": false,
 5      "displayName": "AKSAADServer",
 6      "errorUrl": null,
 7      "groupMembershipClaims": "All",
 8      "optionalClaims": null,
 9      "acceptMappedClaims": null,
10      "homepage": "http://AKSAADServer",
11      "informationalUrls": {
12          "privacy": null,
13          "termsOfService": null
14      },
```

5. Generate and save the keys:

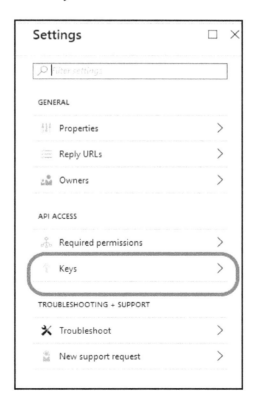

6. Enter the description, set the expiry, and click on **Save**:

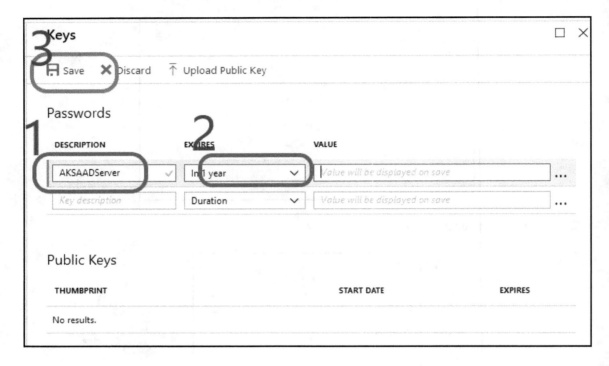

7. Ensure that you save the key value:

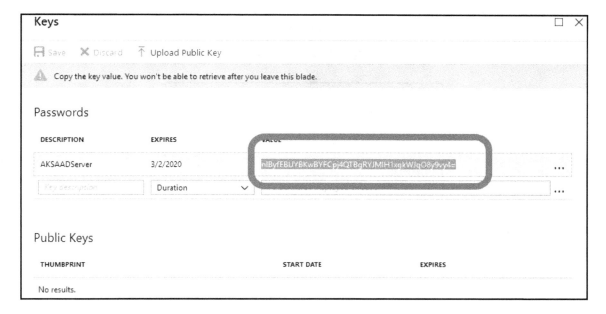

Please make sure that you save the key value somewhere secure.

The following subsections have details on setting up and granting the permissions for the Azure AD application so that it can access the user information from the Azure AD.

Setting the permissions for the application to access user info

We need to set the permissions for the Azure AD server application to be able to access the users in the Azure AD. Perform the following steps:

1. Select **Settings** and go to **Required permissions**:

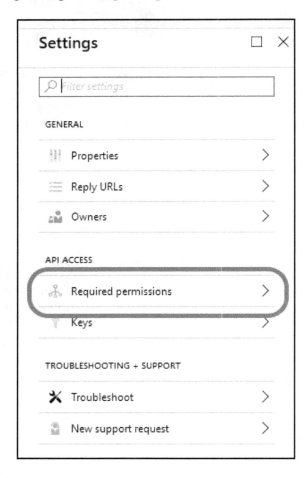

2. Click on **Add** and go to **Select an API**:

3. Select **Microsoft Graph**:

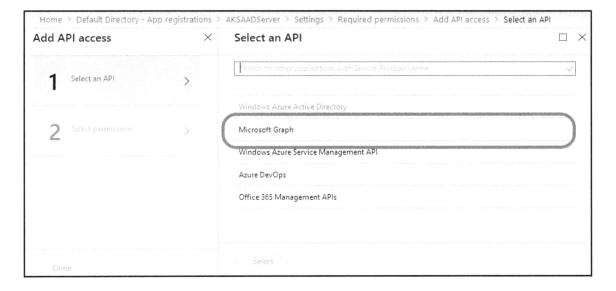

4. Allow the application to read the AAD data:

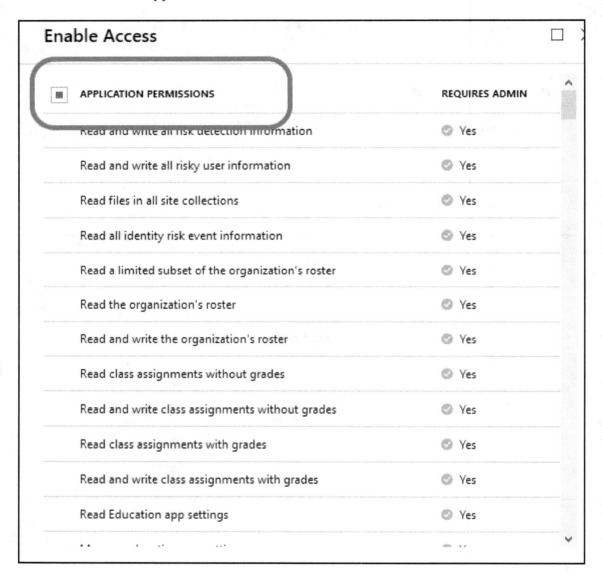

5. Under **Application Permissions**, place a checkmark next to **Read directory data**:

6. Allow **DELEGATED PERMISSIONS** so that the application can read directory data on behalf of the user:

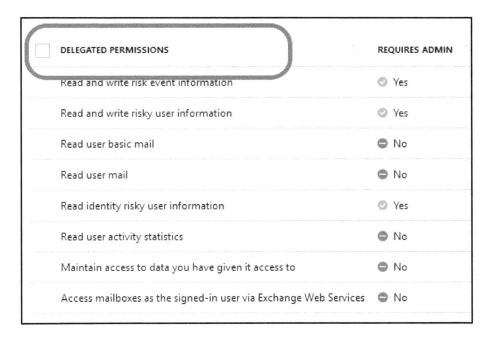

7. Under **DELEGATED PERMISSIONS**, place a checkmark next to **Sign in and read user profile** and **Read directory data**:

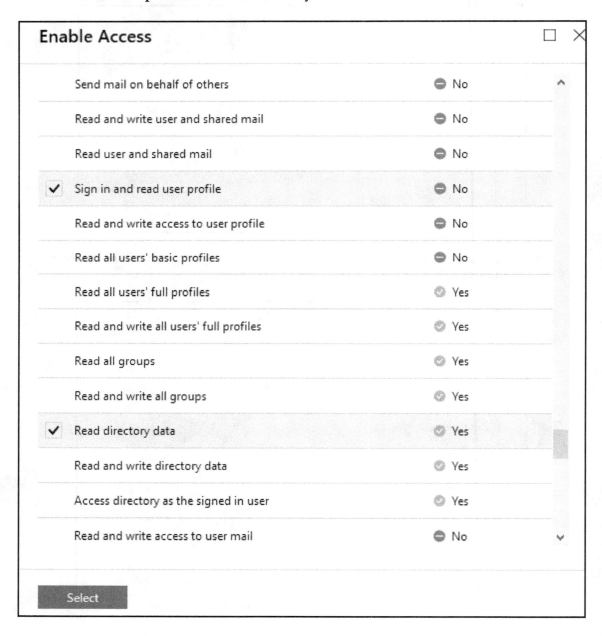

Granting the permissions and noting the application ID

1. Choose **Microsoft Graph** from the list of APIs, then select **Grant Permissions**:

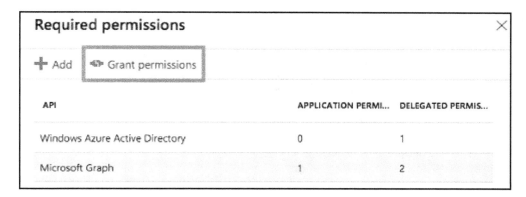

2. Return to the application and take note of the **Application ID**:

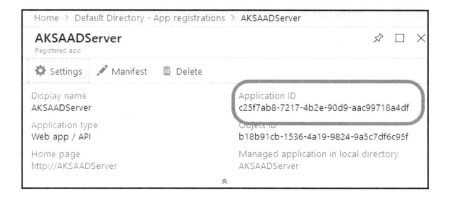

Creating the client application

This application is used when logging into the cluster. The process is similar to the preceding with slight differences. Let's get started:

1. Register the client application:

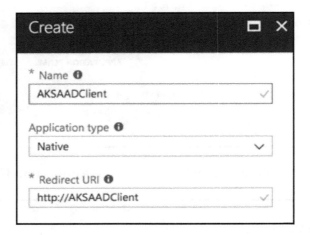

2. Add and grant the required permissions.
3. Give this application the right to access the AAD server application:

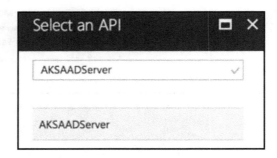

4. Place a checkmark next to the application and click on **Select** and then **Done**:

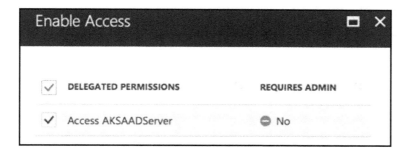

5. Write down the **Application ID**. This will be used as "Client application ID" when creating the cluster:

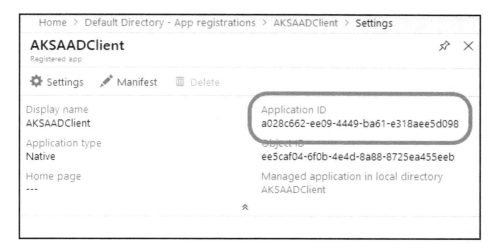

This way we have created a client application ID.

Getting the AAD tenant ID

You can get the ID of your Azure tenant by selecting **Azure Active Directory -> Properties**:

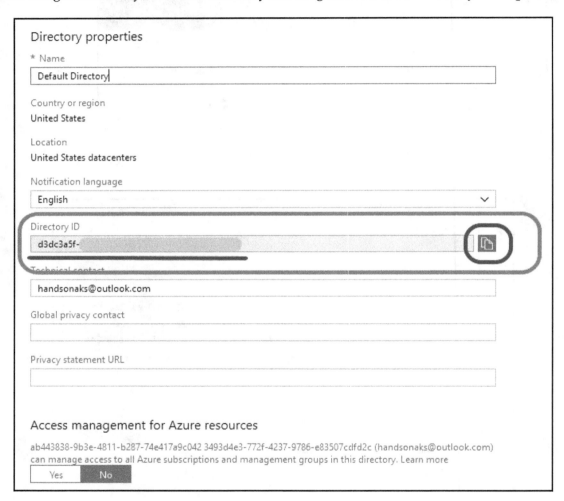

You can get the tenant ID of *any* domain by accessing `https://login.windows.net/`**`<domainname>`**`.onmicrosoft.com/.well-known/openid-configuration`.

For example, for this book, the domain name was handsonaksoutlook: `https://login.windows.net/handsonaksoutlook.onmicrosoft.com/.well-known/openid-configuration`.

Deploying the cluster

On the cloud shell, create a resource group:

```
az group create --name handsonaks-rbac --location eastus
```

Deploy the cluster using the following command on the cloud shell:

```
az aks create \
  --resource-group handsonaks-rbac \
  --name handsonaks-rbac \
  --generate-ssh-keys \
  --aad-server-app-id <server-app-id> \
  --aad-server-app-secret <server-app-secret> \
  --aad-client-app-id <client-app-id> \
  --aad-tenant-id <tenant-id>
```

Your fresh and hot cluster should be ready in 10 minutes or so.

Attaching service roles to AAD users

We will be creating users in our directory and assigning roles to them.

Creating users in your Active Directory

Select Azure **Active Directory->Users** and select **New user**. As shown in the following screenshot:

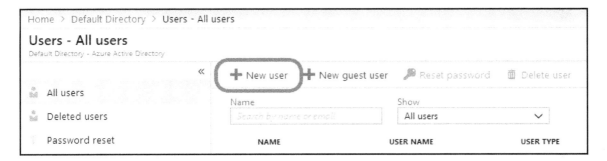

Do not select **New guest user**. Guest users cannot be assigned roles.

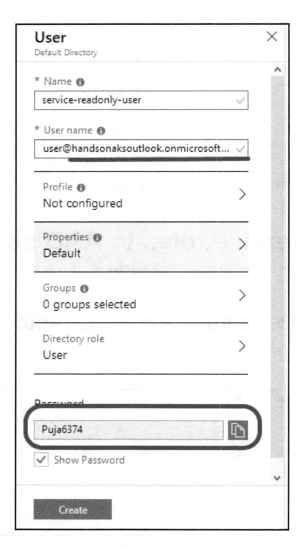

The username has to be in the domain that you are the admin of. In this case, an Outlook account was used and hence the domain name is `handsonaksoutlook.onmicrosoft.com`. Write down the password.

Creating a read-only group and adding the user to it

To demonstrate that you can manage using groups, instead of individual users, let's create a read-only user group and add the new user to the group:

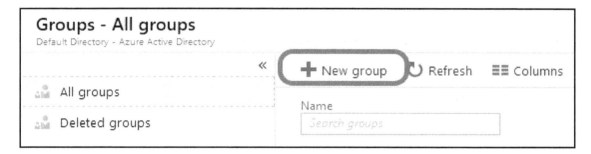

You can select the users when creating the group:

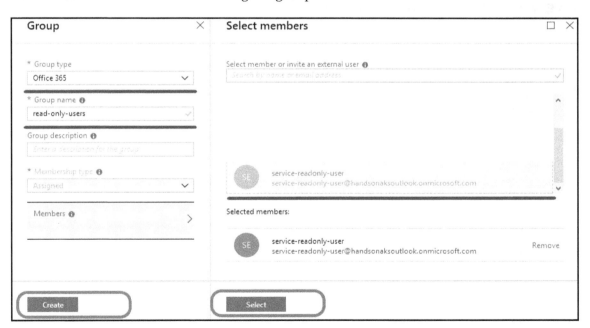

Verifying RBAC

Let's give it a spin by creating the RBAC roles on Kubernetes and checking whether it actually works.

Creating the read-only user role

On the cloud shell, connect to your cluster.

Note that you have to specify --admin so that you can work on your cluster:

```
az aks get-credentials --resource-group handsonaks-rbac --name handsonaks-rbac --admin
```

Creating the cluster-wide, read-only role

Create the following file and save it as cluster-read-only-role.yaml:

```
apiVersion: rbac.authorization.k8s.io/v1
kind: ClusterRole
metadata:
  labels:
  name: read-only
rules:
- apiGroups:
  - ""
  resources: ["*"]
  verbs:
  - get
  - list
  - watch
- apiGroups:
  - extensions
  resources: ["*"]
  verbs:
  - get
  - list
  - watch
- apiGroups:
  - apps
  resources: ["*"]
  verbs:
  - get
```

```
- list
- watch
```

Run the following command to create a cluster-wide role named `read-only` that has read-only permissions across the cluster:

```
kubectl create -f cluster-read-only-role.yaml
```

Binding the role to the AAD group

Create the following file and save it as `readonly-azure-aad-group.yaml`:

```
kind: ClusterRoleBinding
apiVersion: rbac.authorization.k8s.io/v1
metadata:
  name: read-only
roleRef:
  kind: ClusterRole #this must be Role or ClusterRole
  name: read-only # this must match the name of the Role or ClusterRole you
wish to bind to
  apiGroup: rbac.authorization.k8s.io
subjects:
- kind: Group
  apiGroup: rbac.authorization.k8s.io
  name: "<insert the read-only group id here"
```

Run the following command to create the read-only role, but this time access is given to anyone who is present in the group:

```
kubectl create -f readonly-azure-aad-group.yaml
```

The access test

Now, get the credentials as the read-only user.

This time, the "`--admin`" parameter is *not* passed:

```
az aks get-credentials --resource-group handsonaks-rbac --name handsonaks-
rbac
```

Run the following command, just to test RBAC:

```
kubectl get all
```

You will be asked to log in:

```
To sign in, use a web browser to open the page
https://microsoft.com/devicelogin and enter the code BRVBZLAHE to
authenticate.
```

Log in using the `readonly` account username. When you log in the first time, you will be asked to change the password:

```
AKSAADClient



You have signed in to the AKSAADClient application
on your device. You may now close this window.
```

Once you have logged in successfully, you can close the window and you should see the following output:

```
NAME           TYPE         CLUSTER-IP     EXTERNAL-IP    PORT(S)     AGE
kubernetes     ClusterIP    10.0.0.1       <none>         443/TCP     14h
Error from server (Forbidden): horizontalpodautoscalers.autoscaling is
forbidden: User "service-readonly-user@handsonaksoutlook.onmicrosoft.com"
cannot list horizontalpodautoscalers.autoscaling in the namespace "default"
Error from server (Forbidden): jobs.batch is forbidden: User "service-
readonly-user@handsonaksoutlook.onmicrosoft.com" cannot list jobs.batch in
the namespace "default"
Error from server (Forbidden): cronjobs.batch is forbidden: User "service-
readonly-user@handsonaksoutlook.onmicrosoft.com" cannot list cronjobs.batch
in the namespace "default"
```

So we can see most of it except the pod `autoscalers/batch` jobs and `cronjobs`.

Let's see whether we actually have read-only access by trying to delete something, such as a pod:

```
kubectl delete pods/<pod name running in the namespace kube-system> -n
kube-system
```

You will get a Forbidden message:

```
Error from server (Forbidden): pods "heapster-779db6bd48-nvhv9" is
forbidden: User "service-readonly-user@handsonaksoutlook.onmicrosoft.com"
cannot delete pods in the namespace "kube-system"
```

We have ensured that we have access *only* to the user we have given access.

Summary

In this chapter, we learned how to secure your AKS cluster with role-based security by leveraging Azure Active Directory as the authentication provider. We created a service role that lets you assign read-only or read/write access to Kubernetes resources, and we looked at some advanced features. First, we showed you how to create the AAD server application. Then we created the client application. After that, we showed you how to get the AAD tenant ID and deployed the cluster. Once we had the RBAC-enabled solution deployed, we tested the read-only feature by creating users in the Active Directory. We then created a read-only group and added the user to it. We finished the chapter by creating the read-only user role and binding the role to the AAD group of the user.

In the next chapter, you will learn how to authorize Kubernetes cluster applications to connect to other Azure services, such as Azure SQL databases and Event Hubs.

3
Section 3: Leveraging Advanced Azure PaaS Services in Combination with AKS

Having completed this section, the reader should be able to securely access other Azure services, such as databases, Event Hubs, and Azure Functions. Advanced secrets and certificate management using services such as Let's Encrypt will also be familiar to the reader.

The following chapters will be covered in this section:

- Chapter 8, *Connecting an App to an Azure Database - Authorization*
- Chapter 9, *Connecting to Other Azure Services (Event Hub)*
- Chapter 10, *Securing AKS Network Connections*
- Chapter 11, *Serverless Functions*
- Chapter 12, *Next Steps*

8
Connecting an App to an Azure Database - Authorization

This chapter will take you through the process of connecting to an Azure Database. A connection to one or multiple databases can build the backbone for almost every commercial application. Therefore, we will discuss the benefits of using a hosted database versus running StatefulSets on Kubernetes itself. In addition, we will show you aspects of security, backup, **disaster recovery (DR)**, authorization, and audit logging. The independent scaling of the database and the cluster will also be explored. We will break down the discussion of this chapter into the following topics:

- Extending an app to connect to an Azure Database
- Restoring from backup
- Reviewing audit logs
- DR options

Technical requirements

You will require the following tools for this chapter:

- A modern web browser such as Chrome, Firefox, or Edge
- The **role-based access control (RBAC)**-enabled cluster that was deployed in the last chapter and that is still running

Extending an app to connect to an Azure Database

All the examples that we have gone through so far have been self-contained; that is, everything ran inside the Kubernetes cluster. While there is a great advantage to being mostly cloud-agnostic, this is a huge disadvantage when it comes to managing state. Almost any production application has state and is generally stored in a database. In this section, we will launch the WordPress application, but this time we will use an external database managed by Azure.

WordPress backed by Azure MySQL

As with most applications these days, much of the hard work has already been done by the open source community (including those who work for Microsoft). Microsoft has realized that many users would like to use their managed services from Kubernetes, and that they require an easier way of using the same methodologies that are used for Kubernetes deployment. To aid in this effort, they have released Helm charts that use these managed services as a backend (`https://github.com/Azure/helm-charts`). We will be using `https://github.com/Azure/helm-charts/tree/master/wordpress` as a sample application.

First, we will need to install the prerequisites that are described in the following section.

Prerequisites

Since the WordPress sample application requires custom interfacing with Azure services, it requires a little bit more than the normal Helm init and installation that we have explained in previous chapters. We will need to install Open Service Broker for Azure (`https://osba.sh/`).

We will follow the instructions from `https://github.com/Azure/open-service-broker-azure/blob/master/docs/quickstart-aks.md` to install the Open Service Broker for Azure on an Azure Container Service-managed cluster.

Let's start by making a number of changes to add RBAC support for Helm.

Helm with RBAC

Since we have RBAC enabled on the cluster, we need to install Helm with RBAC support:

 It is assumed that the RBAC-enabled cluster that was deployed in the previous chapter is still running.

1. Get the admin credentials by running the following command on Azure Cloud Shell:

```
az aks get-credentials --resource-group handsonaks-rbac --name
handsonaks-rbac --admin
```

2. Get the roles required for Helm by fetching them as follows:

```
kubectl create -f
https://raw.githubusercontent.com/Azure/helm-charts/master/docs/pre
requisities/helm-rbac-config.yaml
```

3. Install Helm using the `tiller` service account:

```
helm init --service-account tiller
```

Deploying the service catalog on the cluster

The service catalog provides the catalog servers that are required for the Open Service Broker. To deploy the service catalog on the cluster, follow these steps:

1. Let's deploy the service catalog by running the following commands:

```
helm repo add svc-cat
https://svc-catalog-charts.storage.googleapis.com
helm install svc-cat/catalog --name catalog --namespace catalog \
    --set apiserver.storage.etcd.persistence.enabled=true \
    --set apiserver.healthcheck.enabled=false \
    --set controllerManager.healthcheck.enabled=false \
    --set apiserver.verbosity=2 \
    --set controllerManager.verbosity=2
```

2. Wait until the service catalog is deployed. You can check this by running the
   following command:

   ```
   helm status catalog
   ```

3. Verify that the AVAILABLE column shows 1 for both the API server and the
   manager:

   ```
   ==> v1beta1/Deployment
   NAME                                     READY  UP-TO-DATE  AVAILABLE
   AGE
   catalog-catalog-apiserver                1/1    1           1
   5h54m
   catalog-catalog-controller-manager 1/1    1           1
   5h54m
   ```

Deploying Open Service Broker for Azure

We need to obtain the subscription ID, tenant ID, client ID, and secrets in order for the
Open Service Broker to launch Azure services on our behalf:

1. Run the following command to obtain the required lists:

   ```
   az account list -o table
   ```

2. Copy your subscription ID and save it in an environment variable:

   ```
   export AZURE_SUBSCRIPTION_ID="<SubscriptionId>"
   ```

3. Create a service principal with RBAC enabled so that it can launch Azure
   services:

   ```
   az ad sp create-for-rbac --name osba-quickstart -o table
   ```

4. Save the values from the command output in the environment variable:

   ```
   export AZURE_TENANT_ID=<Tenant>
   export AZURE_CLIENT_ID=<AppId>
   export AZURE_CLIENT_SECRET=<Password>
   ```

5. Now we can deploy the Open Service Broker, as follows:

```
helm repo add azure
https://kubernetescharts.blob.core.windows.net/azure
helm install azure/open-service-broker-azure --name osba --
namespace osba \
    --set azure.subscriptionId=$AZURE_SUBSCRIPTION_ID \
    --set azure.tenantId=$AZURE_TENANT_ID \
    --set azure.clientId=$AZURE_CLIENT_ID \
    --set azure.clientSecret=$AZURE_CLIENT_SECRETD
```

Deploying WordPress

Following are the steps to deploy WordPress:

1. Run the following command to install WordPress:

```
helm install azure/wordpress --name osba-quickstart --namespace
osba-quickstart
```

2. Run the following command to know when WordPress is ready:

```
kubectl get deploy osba-quickstart-wordpress -n osba-quickstart -w
```

NAME	DESIRED	CURRENT	UP-TO-DATE	AVAILABLE	AGE
osba-quickstart-wordpress	1	1	1	0	1m
...					
osba-quickstart-wordpress	1	1	1	1	2m

In case you run into Not able to schedule pod problem, use the `kubectl edit deploy/osba-quickstart-wordpress -n osba-quickstart` command and set the replicas to 1 (you can refer to Chapter 6, *Monitoring the AKS Cluster and the Application,* for more information).

Securing MySQL

Although many steps are automated for us, this doesn't mean MySQL is production-ready. For instance, the network settings for the MySQL server has the following **AllowAll 0.0.0.0** rule entry in **Connection security**:

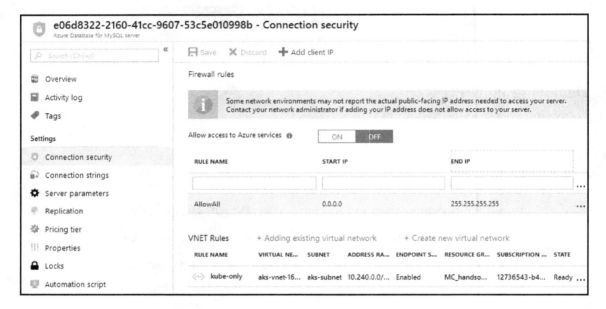

This rule allows a connection to the database from any IP address. As you may have already guessed, this is a serious security hole and is the cause of many data breaches. The good news is that this rule is not required when using AKS. You can add the AKS VNet to the **VNET Rules** section and delete the **AllowAll 0.0.0.0** rule, as shown in the following screenshot:

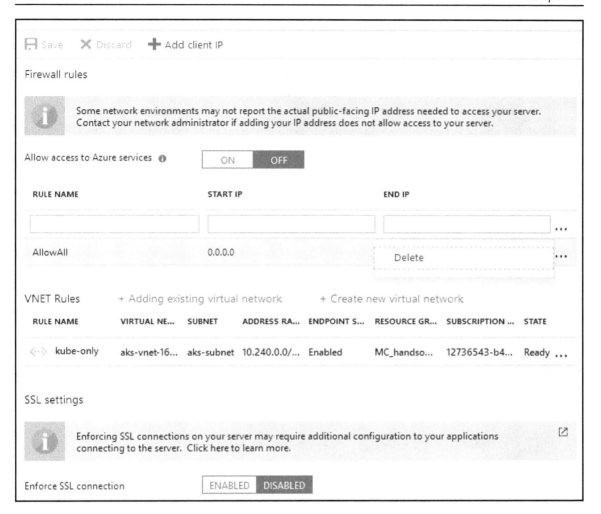

We can reduce the attack surface tremendously by performing this simple change.

Running the WordPress sample with MySQL Database

You can verify that your blog site is available and running by using `SERVICE_IP`, which is obtained by running the following command:

```
echo $(kubectl get svc --namespace osba-quickstart osba-quickstart-
wordpress -o jsonpath='{.status.loadBalancer.ingress[0].ip}')
```

Then, open a web browser and go to `http://<SERVICE_IP>/`.

We have launched a WordPress site that is backed by an Azure-managed database. We have also secured it by modifying the firewall. In the next section, we will go through the advantages of letting Azure manage your database.

Restoring from backup

When you run a database within your Kubernetes cluster, **high availability** (**HA**), backup, and DR are your responsibilities. Setting up cron jobs to take backups and store them separately, and also ensuring that the instance is up and running, makes this a complicated operation. As a developer or an operator, running MySQL in production will not be your core competency and it is also unlikely to be for your company. Just as we don't manage our own Kubernetes cluster (we use the managed Kubernetes service), for production, we recommend that you keep life simple by using the managed option.

 You can refer to `https://docs.microsoft.com/en-us/azure/mysql/`
`concepts-backup` to find up-to-date information on the backup frequency, replication, and restore options.

Performing a restore

For testing the restore capabilities, let's add a few entries on the WordPress blog. Let's assume that during an update, the database was corrupted, and so we want to do a point-in-time restore.

All you have to do is click on **Restore** and choose the point in time from which you want to perform the restore, as shown in the following screenshot:

Finally, press **OK**; after approximately 15 minutes, the MySQL service should be restored.

Connecting WordPress to the restored database

Azure MySQL restore creates a new instance of the database. To make our WordPress installation connect to the restored database, we need to modify the Kubernetes deployment files. Ideally, you will modify the Helm values file and perform a Helm upgrade; however, that is beyond the scope of this book:

1. From the Azure Portal, note down the **Server name**, as shown in the following screenshot:

2. Also, modify **Connection security** to allow the cluster to talk to the restored database, as shown in the following screenshot:

To verify the restore, add a few entries on the blog. On restore, these entries should not be present.

Modifying the host setting in WordPress deployment

In this section, we will show you how to modify the deployment by examining the deployment file (by using `kubectl describe deploy/...`):

1. You can see that the host value is obtained from the secret, as follows:

```
MARIADB_HOST: <set to the key 'host' in secret 'osba-quickstart-
wordpress-mysql-secret'>
```

2. To set secrets, we need the `base64` value. Obtain the `base64` value of the server name by running the following command:

```
echo <restored db server name> | base64
```

Note the `base64` value.

3. Get the URI value by running the following command:

```
kc get -o yaml secrets/osba-quickstart-wordpress-mysql-secret -n
osba-quickstart
```

4. Get the value for URI and decode it using the following command:

```
echo 'base64 -uri value' | base64 -d
```

5. Change the server name in the URI string
   from `mysql://username:password@`**`<orig-db-name>`**`.mysql.database.azure.com:3306/k9mhjialu3?useSSL=true&requireSSL=true` to `mysql://<sameusername>:<same password>@`**`<restored-db-name>`**`.mysql.database.azure.com:3306/k9mhjialu3?useSSL=true&requireSSL=true`.

6. Get the encoded value again by running the following command:

```
echo 'new uri' | base64 -w 0
```

Note down the new URI value.

7. Run the following command to set the host to the new value:

```
kubectl edit secrets/osba-quickstart-wordpress-mysql-secret -n
osba-quickstart-wordpress
```

8. Set the value of the host to the Base64 value that you noted down when encoding the restored MySQL server name:

```
apiVersion: v1
data:
  database: azltaGppYWx1Mw==
  host: <change this value>
  password:...
  uri: <change this value>
```

9. Save the preceding file by hitting *Esc* and then :wq.

   Even though we have reset the secret value, this doesn't mean that our server will automatically pick up the new value.

10. There are many ways to do it, but we are going to use scaling. Scale down the number of replicas by running the following command:

    ```
    kc scale --replicas=0 deploy/osba-quickstart-wordpress -n osba-quickstart
    ```

Due to problems with attaching and detaching storage, we have to wait for at least 15 minutes for the storage to become detached.

11. After waiting 15 minutes, scale the replicas up again:

    ```
    kc scale --replicas=1 deploy/osba-quickstart-wordpress -n osba-quickstart
    ```

    Even though, in theory, the preceding should work, if you run the kubectl logs on the WordPress pod, you will see that it is still using the old server name.

    This means that logs– has to come from the mounted volume. Running grep -R 'original server name' * on the pod by using kubectl exec shows that the values are actually stored in /bitnami/wordpress/wp-config.php.

12. Open the file and put in the restored database name. Scale the replicas up and down (after waiting for 15 minutes). It might be easier to create a new **persistent volume claim (PVC)**.

The blog logs will show that it is connecting to the restored database.

Reviewing audit logs

When you run the database on the Kubernetes cluster, it is very difficult to get audit logs should something goes wrong. You need a robust way of dynamically setting the audit level depending on the scenario. You also have to ensure that the logs are shipped outside the cluster. Unless you have RBAC enabled, and that the RBAC logs are correlated, it is difficult to determine whether anyone has made changes to the database server settings.

A managed Azure Database solves the preceding issues by providing a robust auditing mechanism via the Azure Portal.

Azure Database audits

A very powerful tool for troubleshooting is the Azure Database audit logs. You can review the basic logs by looking at the **Activity log**:

The **Activity log** provides very valuable information in retracing the activities that have been performed. Another option is to leverage the advanced logs that are available, which we can obtain by enabling **Server logs**, as shown in the following screenshot. First, go to the logs settings, and then click on **Click here to enable logs and configure log parameters**:

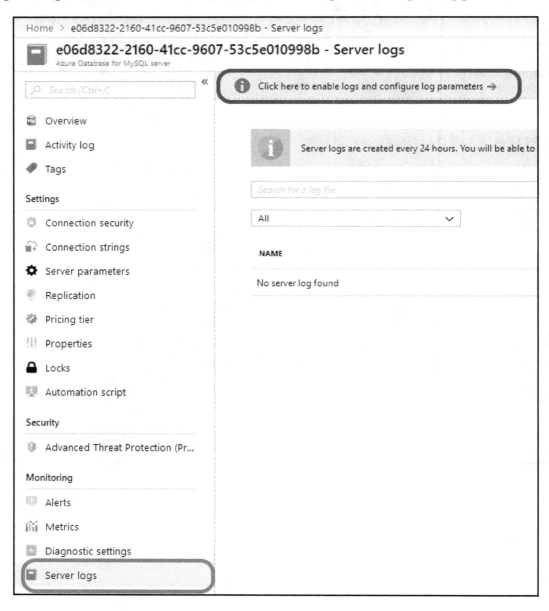

For our example, we will enable monitoring for performance issues by enabling the `log_slow...` statements, as shown in the following screenshot:

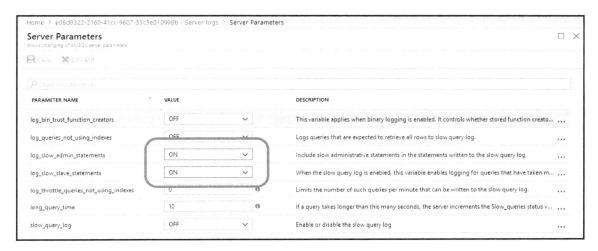

DR options

Depending on your **Service Level Agreement** (**SLA**) and DR needs, you can add replicas to your MySQL server, as shown in the following screenshot:

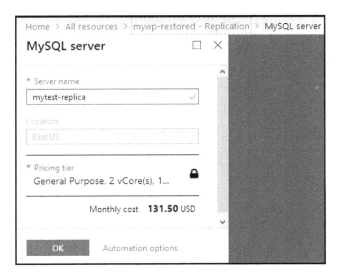

A full list of backup, restore, and replication options are documented at `https://docs.microsoft.com/en-us/azure/mysql/concepts-backup` and `https://docs.microsoft.com/en-us/azure/mysql/concepts-read-replicas`.

Azure SQL HADR options

Naturally, the options are much better when you use Azure SQL Database than with MySQL. Brief highlights of all the options are listed and users are encouraged to choose their database server based on their own needs. You can create a test database to see the options yourself, as shown in the following screenshot:

The advanced options are shown in the following screenshot:

We only want to highlight two of the advanced options that we looked at in the previous section for MySQL, which are also available with Azure SQL Database:

- **Active Directory (AD) admin**: You can connect your company's Azure AD to provide controlled access to the databases.
- **Auditing**: Fine-grained auditing, even for row-level access, can be set.

Another great feature is that **Geo-Replication** can also be easily added, as shown in the following screenshot:

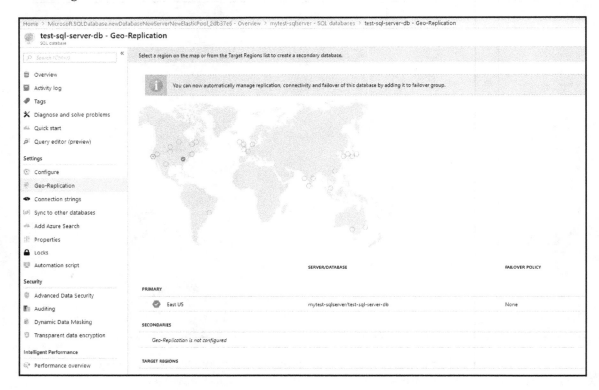

Summary

This chapter focused on working with the WordPress sample solution that leverages a MySQL database as a data store. We started by showing you how to set up the cluster to connect the MySQL database by installing the Open Service Broker for Azure and leveraging the RBAC-enabled Helm tool. We then showed you how to install a MySQL database and drastically minimize the attack surface by changing the default configuration to not allow public access to the database. Then, we discussed how to restore the database from a backup and how to leverage the audit logs for troubleshooting. Finally, we discussed how to configure the solution for DR, and so satisfy your organization's DR needs by using Azure SQL geo-replication.

In the next chapter, you will learn how to implement microservices on AKS, including by using Event Hubs for loosely-coupled integration between the applications.

Connecting to Other Azure Services (Event Hub)

9

Event-based integration is a key pattern for implementing microservices. In this chapter, you will learn how to how to implement microservices on AKS, including how to use Event Hub for loosely coupled integration between the applications. The securing of the communications between microservices will also be introduced to the reader. Microservices, when implemented with the correct organization/support in place, help businesses develop a growth mindset in their teams. DevOps maturity is crucial in making the digital transformation of companies a reality. You, as a developer and/or an engineer responsible for site reliability, will learn how to deploy them, and also how to leverage Azure Event Hub to store events. As you will learn in this chapter, events-based integration is one of the key differentiators between monolithic and microservice-based applications. We will cover the following topics in brief:

- Introducing to microservices
- Deploying a set of microservices
- Using Azure Event Hubs

Technical requirements

You will need to use a modern browser, such as Firefox, Chrome, or Edge.

Introducing to microservices

Microservices are an architectural pattern for organizing your application according to business domains. For more information on microservices, please see `https://martinfowler.com/articles/microservices.html`. Classic examples that are usually provided for microservices are how customer, movies, and recommendation services are implemented. Customer service simply deals with customer details, and has no information about movies. The movies service deals with movie details and nothing more. The recommendation engine service deals with recommendations only, and, given a movie title, will return the movie that are closely related.

One of the main selling points of microservices is strengthen independence. Services are designed to be small enough (hence the name *micro*) to handle the needs of a business domain. As they are small, they can be made self-contained and independently testable, and so are independently releasable. With the use of proper contract tests, each team can rollout their release on their own schedule, without the need for handoffs.

Graceful degradation is another benefit of microservices. If the recommendation engine is not functioning, the customer will still be able to log in and watch movies.

Independent scaling is another benefit that is mostly useful for systems with heavy users. In our example, if more requests are coming in for recommendations, our service can be scaled up without scaling up other services.

Each service can be built with the right language of choice. For high performance, the Rust language can be used, or the development team might even be more comfortable developing in Python. As long as they expose REST services, they can be deployed with services written in any other language.

Blue/green deployment and rolling updates are also made possible by the use of microservices. You can deploy the upgraded service and check whether or not they are working, and then push all the new requests to the upgraded service. The requests to the old service can be drained. The preceding deployment is called blue/green deployment. If something goes wrong, the upgraded service is downscaled, and the customers experience almost no downtime. Rolling updates are similar, where the old pods are slowly replaced with the new pods and the process is reversed if something goes wrong.

Since services are kept small, they can be rewritten quickly in case the initial implementation is wrong. Composable services, such as aggregator services, can be built on top of existing services to speed up development. Microservices bring back the old Unix philosophy of doing one thing, and doing it well. Composability is the method of integrating services rather than stuffing everything in one service.

Microservices are no free lunch

With all the advantages mentioned previously, as described in `http://highscalability.com/blog/2014/4/8/microservices-not-a-free-lunch.html` by Benjamin Wootton (`https://twitter.com/benjaminwootton`), CTO of Contino (`http://contino.co.uk/`), without enough DevOps maturity and developer awareness of the difficulties encountered in a distributed system, microservices will not be worthwhile for a business. Even though it is slightly old, the warnings mentioned in the article still hold.

Many organizations that promote microservices now, such as Amazon, Netflix, and eBay, had monolithic applications generating boatloads of money for years before they started migrating toward microservices. Having a business driver is the number one requirement for thinking about microservices.

Microservices require a high degree of software developmental maturity for it to be implemented correctly. Architects who understand the domain very well have to follow domain-driven design principles to ensure that each service is bounded and cohesive.

Developers must be aware of deployment issues, such as the backward compatibility of their services, and have to build semantic versioning in their service. Automated tests, including contract tests, are crucial to ensure that the services don't break running systems. Services should be developed in a cloud native fashion that includes retries while trying to connect to dependent services.

CI/CD tools must be present that build and deploy the integrated solution continuously. The infrastructure to create environments on demand and maintain them is required for continuous delivery. Enough skill to automate environment setup to ensure that automated tests can be run reliably is required.

Running distributed systems is hard. Pathological failures can occur anywhere (application, network, storage, memory), and with systems running independently it would be very hard to set up and diagnose.

Debugging asynchronous systems is not an easy skill without the right tools. Operators with maturity are required that can correlate events in logs present in multiple locations.

As long as you are aware of the challenges, microservices can be implemented in any organization. The key idea is to get both top and bottom buy-in with realistic expectations. Then you can implement it in stages with non-critical, but highly visible, services.

Kubernetes and microservices

As we have seen, microservices are not a prerequisite for using Kubernetes. Kubernetes will launch and run your monolithic applications, as well as any microservices.

The reverse cannot generally be said, meaning that Kubernetes has almost become a prerequisite for microservices. The challenges mentioned in the previous section are the main reasons for learning and implementing a complex system like Kubernetes.

Kubernetes allows migration toward microservices at a speed that is comfortable for organizations. It allows CI/CD, with service discovery, scaling, and roll-out support. Now that we've got a fair idea about microservices, let's now learn how to deploy a set of microservices.

Deploying a set of microservices

We will be deploying a set of microservices called a social network. The service is composed of two main service, users and friends. The users service stores all the users in its own data store. The friends service stores the user's friends. The events of adding a user/adding a friend are sent to a recommendation service backed by a graph database that is then used to query relationships between users. You can query the graph database with questions, such as *give me the common friends of user X and user Y*.

In the following section, you will do the following:

- Use Helm to deploy a sample microservice-based application
- Test the service by sending events and watch objects being created and updated

Deploying Helm

First, we will deploy this service as is with the use of the local Kafka instance that acts as the event broker.

1. On Azure Cloud Shell, type the following:

    ```
    # original code forked from
    https://github.com/kbastani/event-sourcing-microservices-example.gi
    t
    git clone
    https://github.com/gshiva/event-sourcing-microservices-example.git
    cd event-sourcing-microservices-example
    ```

2. We will use Kafka and ZooKeeper charts from `bitnami`, so let's add the required `helm repo`:

```
helm repo add bitnami https://charts.bitnami.com
helm repo add incubator
https://kubernetes-charts-incubator.storage.googleapis.com
```

3. Let's update the dependencies to make the dependent charts available:

```
helm dep update deployment/helm/social-network
helm dep update deployment/helm/friend-service
helm dep update deployment/helm/user-service
helm dep update deployment/helm/recommendation-service
```

4. Next, deploy the microservices:

```
helm install --namespace social-network --name social-network --set
fullNameOverride=social-network \
  deployment/helm/social-network
```

5. Check the status of the deployment using the following command:

```
kubectl get pods -w -n social-network
```

6. Wait for about 15-30 minutes until all of the services are up and running. This service does not implement any security, so we use local port forwarding to access the service:

```
kubectl --namespace social-network port-forward svc/edge-service
9000
```

7. Test the services by running the following command:

```
# Generates a 15 person social network using serial API calls
sh ./deployment/sbin/generate-serial.sh
```

We have implemented a microservice-based application in a few commands. We have also seen how port forwarding helps in testing applications locally without having to log on to the nodes. The testing application script shows that even a distributed system can easily be tested, given some upfront work.

The next section, we will move away from storing events in the cluster and storing them in Azure Event Hub. By leveraging recently added Kafka support on Azure Event Hubs, and switching to using a more production-ready event store, we will see that the process is straightforward.

Using Azure Event Hubs

Running Kafka locally is OK for demo purposes, but not suitable for production use. The same reasons why you wouldn't want to run your own database server are why you would avoid running and maintaining your own Kafka instance. Azure Event Hub has added support for the Kafka protocol, so with minor modifications, we can update our application from using local Kafka instance to the scalable Azure Event Hub instance.

In the following sections, we will do the following:

- Create the Azure Event Hub via the portal and gather the required details to connect our microservice-based application.
- Modify the Helm chart to use the newly created Azure Event Hub.

Creating the Azure Event Hub

Perform the following steps to create the Azure Event Hub:

1. To create the Azure Event Hub on Azure portal, search for event hub, shown as follows:

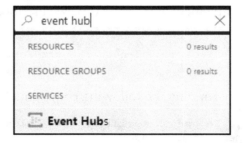

2. Click on **Event Hubs**.
3. On the **Event Hubs** tab, click on **Add**:

4. Fill in the details as follows. For Kafka support, the `Standard` tier must be used:

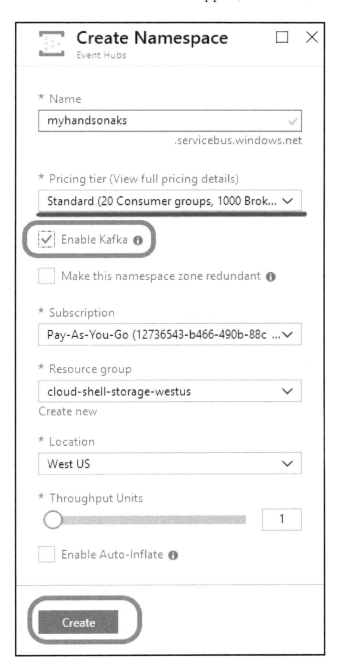

5. Once the Event Hubs is created, select it, as shown in the following screenshot:

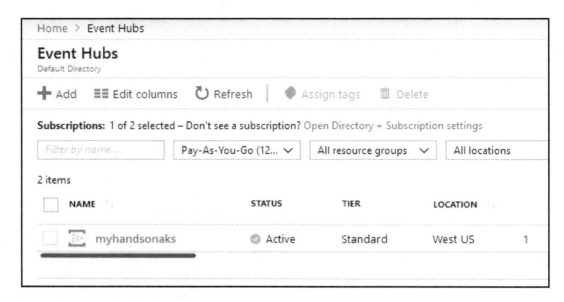

6. Click on the **Shared access policies | RootManageSharedAccessKey** and copy the **Connection string-primary key**, as shown in the following screenshot:

Using Azure portal, we have created the Azure Event Hub that can store and process our events as they are generated. We need to gather the connection strings so that we can hook up our microservice-based application.

Updating the Helm files

We are going to switch the microservice deployment from using the local Kafka instance to using the Azure-hosted, Kafka-compatible Event Hub instance:

1. First, let's delete the local deployment:

   ```
   helm del --purge social-network
   ```

2. Modify the `./deployment/helm/user-service/templates/deployment.yaml` file to change line 32 until the `name: SPRING_PROFILES_ACTIVE` line:

   ```
   - name: SPRING_CLOUD_STREAM_KAFKA_BINDER_BROKERS
     value: "<your eventhub name>.servicebus.windows.net:9093"
   - name: SPRING_CLOUD_STREAM_KAFKA_BINDER_DEFAULT_BROKER_PORT
     value: "9093"
   - name:
   SPRING_CLOUD_STREAM_KAFKA_BINDER_CONFIGURATION_SECURITY_PROTOCOL
     value: "SASL_SSL"
   - name:
   SPRING_CLOUD_STREAM_KAFKA_BINDER_CONFIGURATION_SASL_MECHANISM
     value: "PLAIN"
   - name:
   SPRING_CLOUD_STREAM_KAFKA_BINDER_CONFIGURATION_SASL_JAAS_CONFIG
     value:
   'org.apache.kafka.common.security.plain.PlainLoginModule required
   username="$ConnectionString" password="Endpoint=sb://<youreventhub name>...
   copy the entire connection string that you copied from azure portal'
   ```

   The modified file will have a section that is similar to the following:

   ```
   - name: SPRING_CLOUD_STREAM_KAFKA_BINDER_BROKERS
     value: "myhandsonaks.servicebus.windows.net:9093"
   - name: SPRING_CLOUD_STREAM_KAFKA_BINDER_DEFAULT_BROKER_PORT
     value: "9093"
   - name:
   SPRING_CLOUD_STREAM_KAFKA_BINDER_CONFIGURATION_SECURITY_PROTOCOL
     value: "SASL_SSL"
   - name:
   SPRING_CLOUD_STREAM_KAFKA_BINDER_CONFIGURATION_SASL_MECHANISM
     value: "PLAIN"
   ```

```
        - name:
SPRING_CLOUD_STREAM_KAFKA_BINDER_CONFIGURATION_SASL_JAAS_CONFIG
        value:
'org.apache.kafka.common.security.plain.PlainLoginModule required
username="$ConnectionString" password="Endpoint=sb://handsonaks-
serverless.servicebus.windows.net/;SharedAccessKeyName=RootManageSharedAcce
ssKey;SharedAccessKey=eJ7l5CMBiBnL5gsELsWjWZ4W+liOgXIUH4Pj2wFJugI="
```

3. The same changes have to be made to the following files:

```
./deployment/helm/friend-service/templates/deployment.yaml
./deployment/helm/recommendation-service/templates/deployment.yaml
```

4. Disable the Kafka deployment by setting the `enabled:` value to `false` in `deployment/helm/social-network/values.yaml`:

```
nameOverride: social-network
fullNameOverride: social-network

kafka:
  enabled: false
```

5. Run the deployment as follows:

```
helm install --namespace social-network --name social-network --set
fullNameOverride=social-network    deployment/helm/social-network
```

6. Wait for all the pods to be up, and then run the following command to verify that the install worked:

```
# port forward the service locally
kubectl --namespace social-network port-forward svc/edge-service
9000 &
# Generates a 15 person social network using serial API calls
bash ./deployment/sbin/generate-serial.sh
```

7. You can see the activity on the Azure portal in the following screenshot:

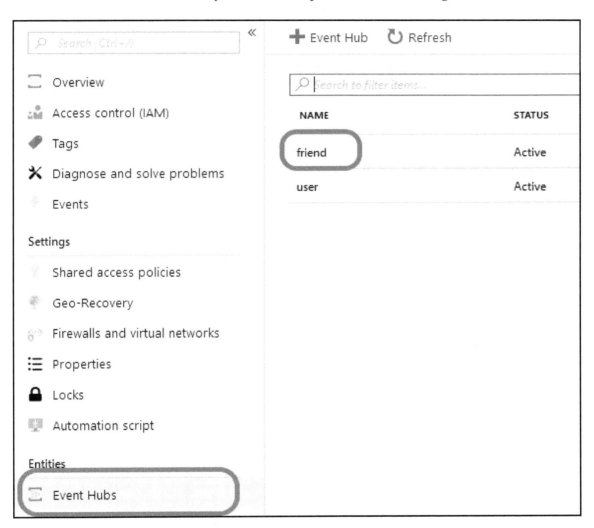

Clicking on the **friend** Event Hub and then **Metrics**, we can see the number of messages that came through and how many came over time (you have to **Add** the **Incoming Messages** metric with the **EntityName = 'friend'** filter), as shown in the following screenshot:

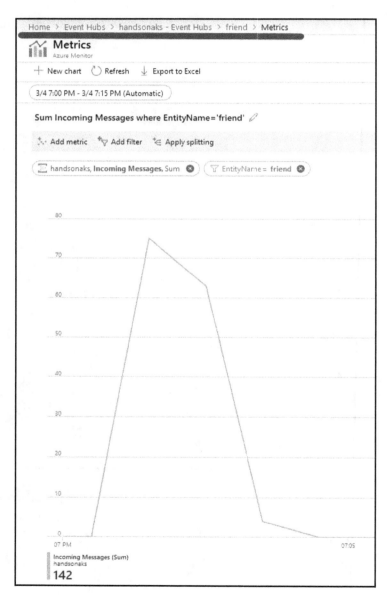

Summary

We started this chapter by covering microservices, their benefits and their trade-offs. Following this, we went on to deploy a set of microservices called social network, where we used Helm to deploy a sample microservice-based application. We were able to test the service by sending events and watching objects being created and updated. Finally, we covered the storing of events in Azure Event Hub using Kafka support, and we were able to gather the required details to connect our microservice-based application and modify the Helm chart. The next chapter will cover cluster and port security using secret objects provided by Kubernetes.

10
Securing AKS Network Connections

Loose lips sink ships is a phrase that describes how easy it can be to jeopardize the security of a Kubernetes-managed cluster (*Kubernetes*, by the way, is Greek for *helmsman of a ship*). If your cluster is left open with the wrong ports or services exposed, or plain text is used for secrets in application definitions, bad actors can take advantage of this lax security and do pretty much whatever they want in your cluster.

In this chapter, we will explore Kubernetes secrets in more depth. You will learn about different secrets backends and how to use them. You'll get a brief introduction to service mesh concepts, and you'll be able to follow along with a practical example.

The following topics will be covered briefly in this chapter:

- SSH secrets management
- The Istio service mesh at your service

Technical requirements

You will require a modern browser, such as Chrome, Firefox, or Edge, for this chapter.

Setting up secrets management

All production applications require some secret information to function. Kubernetes has a pluggable secrets backend to manage these secrets. Kubernetes also provides multiple ways of using the secrets in your deployment. The ability to manage secrets and properly use the secrets backend will make your services resistant to attacks.

We have used secrets in all our deployments in previous chapters. Mostly, we passed the secrets as a string in some kind of variable, or Helm took care of creating the secrets for us. In Kubernetes, secrets are a resource just like pods and replica sets. There are no cluster-wide secrets, which can cause a number of long debugging sessions. Secrets have to be (re)created in all the namespaces where you want to use them. In this section, we'll learn how to create, decode, and use our own secrets.

Creating your own secrets

Kubernetes provides two ways of creating secrets, as follows:

- Creating secrets from files
- Creating secrets from YAML and JSON definitions

Using any of the preceding methods, you can create three types of secrets:

- **Generic secrets**: These can be created using literal values in addition to the preceding two methods.
- **Docker-registry credentials**: These are used to pull images from the private registry.
- **TLS certificates**: These are used to store SSL certificates.

Creating secrets from files

We'll begin by using the file method of creating secrets. Let's say that you need to store a URL and a secret token for accessing an API. To achieve this, you'll need to follow these steps:

1. Store the URL in `apiurl.txt`, as follows:

   ```
   echo "https://my-secret-url-location.topsecret.com" > secreturl.txt
   ```

2. Store the token in another file, as follows:

   ```
   echo '/x~Lhx\nAz!,;.Vk%[#n+";9p%jGF6[' > secrettoken.txt
   ```

3. Let Kubernetes create the secrets from the files, as follows:

   ```
   kubectl create secret generic myapi-url-token --from-
   file=./secreturl.txt --from-file=./secrettoken.txt
   ```

The most interesting argument in the preceding command is the secret type, which we specify as `generic`. There are three secret types defined in Kubernetes:

- `docker-registry`: This is used with the Docker registry; this is very important when you have to pull images from a private repository.
- `generic`: This is the one that we used previously; it creates secrets from files, directories, or literal values.
- `tls`: This is used to store SSL certificates that, for example, can be used in ingress.

The command should return the following output:

```
secret/myapi-url-token created
```

4. We can check whether the secrets were created in the same way as any other Kubernetes resource by using the `get` command:

```
kubectl get secrets
```

This command will return the following output:

```
NAME                TYPE                                   DATA   AGE
defa...      kubernetes.io/service-account-token    3      4d2h
myapi-url-token           Opaque                       2      2m14s
```

Opaque means that, from Kubernetes' perspective, the schema of the contents are unknown. It is an arbitrary key-value pair with no constraints, as opposed to the Docker-registry TLS secrets that will be verified as having the required details.

5. For more details about the secrets, you can also run the `describe` command:

```
kubectl describe secrets/myapi-url-token
```

Notice that you give the token name if you only need a specific secret value. `kubectl describe secrets` will give more details on all the secrets in a namespace.

You will get the following output:

```
Name:           myapi-url-token
Namespace:      default
Labels:         <none>
Annotations:    <none>
```

```
Type:  Opaque

Data
====
secrettoken.txt:  32 bytes
secreturl.txt:    45 bytes
```

Note that both the preceding commands did not display the actual secret values.

6. To get the secrets, run the following command:

```
kubectl get -o yaml secrets/myapi-url-token
```

You will get the following output:

```
apiVersion: v1
data:
  secrettoken.txt: L3h+TGh4XG5BeiEsOy5WayVbI24rIjs5cCVqR0Y2Wwo=
  secreturl.txt:
aHR0cHM6Ly9teS1zZWNyZXQtdXJsLWxvY2F0aW9uLnRvcHNlY3JldC5jb20K
kind: Secret
...
```

The data is stored as key-value pairs, with the filename as the key and the base64encoded contents of the file as the value.

7. The preceding values are base64 encoded. To get the actual values, run the following command:

```
#get the token value
echo 'L3h+TGh4XG5BeiEsOy5WayVbI24rIjs5cCVqR0Y2Wwo=' | base64 -d
```

You will get the value that was originally entered, as follows:

```
/x~Lhx\nAz!,;.Vk%[#n+";9p%jGF6[
```

8. Similarly, for the url value, you can run the following command:

```
#get the url value
echo 'aHR0cHM6Ly9teS1zZWNyZXQtdXJsLWxvY2F0aW9uLnRvcHNlY3JldC5jb20K'
| base64 -d
```

You will get the originally entered url value, as follows:

```
https://my-secret-url-location.topsecret.com
```

In this section, we were able to encode the URL with a secret token and get the actual secret values back using files.

Creating secrets manually using files

We will create the same secrets as in the previous section, only manually, by following these steps:

1. First, we need to encode the secrets to base64, as follows:

```
# encode the token to base64
# -w 0 options ensures that in case the string goes more
# than 80 chars no column wrapping is done
echo '/x~Lhx\nAz!,;.Vk%[#n+";9p%jGF6[' | base64 -w 0
```

You will get the following value:

L3h+TGh4XG5BeiEsOy5WayVbI24rIjs5cCVqROY2Wwo=

You might notice that this is the same value that was present when we got the yaml definition of the secret.

2. Similarly, for the url value, we can get the base64 encoded value, as shown in the following code block:

```
echo 'https://my-secret-url-location.topsecret.com' | base64 -w 0
```
aHR0cHM6Ly9teS1zZWNyZXQtdXJsLWxvY2F0aW9uLnRvcHNlY3JldC5jb20K

3. We can now create the secret definition manually; then, save the file as myfirstsecret.yaml:

```
apiVersion: v1
kind: Secret
metadata:
  name: myapiurltoken
type: Opaque
data:
  url: aHR0cHM6Ly9teS1zZWNyZXQtdXJsLWxvY2F0aW9uLnRvcHNlY3JldC5jb20K
  token: L3h+TGh4XG5BeiEsOy5WayVbI24rIjs5cCVqROY2Wwo=
```

kind tells us that this is a secret; the name value is myapiurltoken, and type is Opaque (from Kubernetes' perspective, values are unconstrained key-value pairs). The data section has the actual data in the form of keys, such as url and token, followed by the encoded values.

4. Now we can create the secrets in the same way as any other Kubernetes resource by using the create command:

```
kubectl create -f myfirstsecret.yaml
kubectl get secrets
```

```
NAME                TYPE              DATA    AGE
defau...            kubernetes.io/..  3       4d5h
myapi-url-token     Opaque            2       167m
myapiurltoken       Opaque            2       25m
```

5. You can double-check that the secrets are the same, by using `kubectl get -o yaml secrets/myapiurltoken` in the same way that we described in the previous section.

Creating generic secrets using literals

The third method of creating secrets is by using the literal method. To do this, run the following command:

```
kubectl create secret generic my-api-secret-literal --from-literal=url=https://my-secret-url-location.topsecret.com --from-literal=token='/x~Lhx\nAz!,;.Vk%[#n+";9p%jGF6['
```

We can verify that the secret was created by running the following command.

```
kubectl get secrets
```

This will give us the following output:

```
NAME                     TYPE        DATA    AGE
...
my-api-secret-literal    Opaque      2       45s
myapi-url-token          Opaque      2       3h
mysecret                 Opaque      2       39m
```

Thus we have created secrets using literal values in addition to the preceding two methods.

Creating the Docker registry key

Connecting to a private Docker registry is a necessity in production environments. Since this use case is so common, Kubernetes has provided mechanisms to create the connection:

```
kubectl create secret docker-registry <secret-name> --docker-server=<your-registry-server> --docker-username=<your-name> --docker-password=<your-pword> --docker-email=<your-email>
```

The first parameter is the secret type, which is `docker-registry`. Then, you give the secret a name; for example, `regcred`. The other parameters are the Docker server (`https://index.docker.io/v1/` for Docker Hub), your username, password, and email.

You can retrieve the secret in the same way as other secrets by using `kubectl` to access secrets.

Creating the tls secret

To create a `tls` secret that can be used in ingress definitions, we use the following command:

```
kubectl create secret tls <secret-name> --key <ssl.key> --cert <ssl.crt>
```

The first parameter is `tls` to set the secret type, and then the `key` value and the actual `certificate` value. These files are usually obtained from your certificate registrar.

 If you want to generate your own secret, you can run the following command:
`openssl req -x509 -nodes -days 365 -newkey rsa:2048 -keyout /tmp/ssl.key -out /tmp/ssl.crt -subj "/CN=foo.bar.com"`

Using your secrets

Kubernetes offers the following two ways to mount your secrets:

- Mounting as environment variables
- Mounting as files

Secrets as environment variables

Secrets are referenced in the pod definition under the `containers` and `env` sections. We will use the secrets that we previously defined in a pod, and learn how to use them in an application:

1. Save the following configuration in a file called `pod-with-env-secrets.yaml`:

```
apiVersion: v1
kind: Pod
metadata:
  name: secret-using-env
spec:
  containers:
  - name: nginx
```

```
      image: nginx
      env:
        - name: SECRET_URL
          valueFrom:
            secretKeyRef:
              name: myapi-url-token
              key: secreturl.txt
        - name: SECRET_TOKEN
          valueFrom:
            secretKeyRef:
              name: myapi-url-token
              key: secrettoken.txt
      restartPolicy: Never
```

Under env, we define the env name as SECRET_URL. Then kubernetes gets the value by using the valueFrom. It is referred to a key in the secret data using secretKeyRef with the myapi-url-token name. Finally, take the value present in the secreturl.txt key.

Similarly, we ask the SECRET_TOKEN value to be set by using the value present in the secrettoken.txt key.

2. Let's now create the pod and see whether it really worked:

```
kubectl create -f pod-with-env-secrets.yaml
```

3. Check whether the environment variables are set correctly:

```
kc exec -it secret-using-env bash
root@secret-using-env:/# echo $SECRET_URL
https://my-secret-url-location.topsecret.com
root@secret-using-env:/# echo $SECRET_TOKEN
/x~Lhx\nAz!,;.Vk%[#n+";9p%jGF6[
```

Any application can use the secret values by referencing the appropriate env variables. Please note that both the application and the pod definition have no hardcoded secrets.

Secrets as files

Let's take a look at how to mount the same secrets as files. We will use the following pod definition to demonstrate how this can be done:

```
apiVersion: v1
kind: Pod
metadata:
  name: secret-using-volume
```

```
spec:
  containers:
  - name: nginx
    image: nginx
    volumeMounts:
    - name: secretvolume
      mountPath: "/etc/secrets"
      readOnly: true
  volumes:
  - name: secretvolume
    secret:
      secretName: myapi-url-token
```

The preceding definition tells us that the `volumeMounts` section should mount a volume called `secretvolume`. The `mountPath` where it should be mounted is `/etc/secrets`; additionally, it is `readOnly`.

Note that this is more succinct than the `env` definition, as you don't have to define a name for each and every secret. However, applications need to have a special code to read the contents of the file in order to load it properly. This method is suited for loading entire config files.

Let's see whether the secrets made it through:

1. Save the preceding file as `pod-with-vol-secret.yaml`. Then, create the pod using the following command:

   ```
   kubectl create -f pod-with-vol-secret.yaml
   ```

2. Echo the contents of the files in the mounted volume:

   ```
   kubectl create -f secret-using-volume bash
   ls /etc/secrets/ | xargs -I {}  cat /etc/secrets/{}
   /x~Lhx\nAz!,;.Vk%[#n+";9p%jGF6[
   https://my-secret-url-location.topsecret.com
   ```

 RBAC is very important, even though there is some protection from storing secrets separately. A person who has access to the cluster has access to the secrets that are stored and encrypted with a single master key in the `etcd` data containers. Also, with enough user rights, any secret can be decoded by accessing the pod or using `kubectl get -o yaml secrets/...` method.

The Istio service mesh at your service

We have found a number of ways to secure our pods, but our network connections are still open. Any pod in the cluster can talk to any other pod in the same cluster. As a site reliability engineer, you will want to enforce both ingress and egress rules. As a developer, you don't want to be bothered by it as you won't have information on where your application will be deployed, as well as what is allowed and what is not. If only there was a way that we could run the applications as is, while still specifying network policies.

Enter service mesh—this is defined as the layer that controls service-to-service communication. Just as with microservices, service mesh implementation is not a free lunch. If you don't have hundreds of microservices running, you probably don't need a service mesh. If you decide that you really do need one, you will need to choose one first. There are four popular options, each with its own advantages:

- Linkerd (`https://linkerd.io/`)
- Envoy (`https://www.envoyproxy.io/`)
- Istio (`https://istio.io/`)
- Linkerd2, formerly Conduit (`https://conduit.io/`)

You should choose one service mesh based on your needs, and feel comfortable in the knowledge that, until you hit really high volumes, any one of these solutions will work for you.

We are going to try `istio` for no reason other than its high star rating, at the time of writing, on GitHub (over 15,000). This rating is far higher than any other project.

Installing Istio

Installing `istio` is easy; to do so, follow these steps:

1. Download the `istio` package, as follows:

   ```
   curl -L https://git.io/getLatestIstio | sh -
   cd istio-<release-number>/
   ```

2. Add the `istio` binaries to your path, as follows:

   ```
   export PATH="$PATH:~/istio-<release-number>/bin"
   ```

3. Install `istio` with the default values:

```
helm install install/kubernetes/helm/istio --name istio --namespace
istio-system
```

4. Make sure everything is up and running, as follows:

```
kc get svc -n istio-system
```

We now have `istio` up and running.

Injecting Istio as a sidecar automatically

Istio has the ability to install itself as a sidecar automatically by using labels in the namespace. We can make it function in this way by using the following steps:

1. Let's label the default namespace with the appropriate label, namely, `istio-injection=enabled`:

```
kubectl label namespace default istio-injection=enabled
```

2. Let's launch an application to see whether the sidecar is indeed deployed automatically:

```
kubectl apply -f samples/bookinfo/platform/kube/bookinfo.yaml
```

3. Get the pods running on the default namespace:

```
kubectl get pods
```

4. Run the `describe` command on any one of the pods:

```
kc describe pods/details-<pod id>
```

You can see that the sidecar has indeed been applied:

```
Name:          details-v1-7bcdcc4fd6-xqwjz
Namespace:     default
...
Labels:        app=details
               pod-template-hash=3678770982
               version=v1
Annotations:   sidecar.istio.io/status:
{"version":"887285bb7fa76191bf7f637f283183f0ba057323b078d44c3db4597
8346cbc1a","initContainers":["istio-init"],"containers":["istio-
```

```
proxy"]...
    ...
```

Note that without making any modifications to the underlying application, we were able to get the `istio` service mesh deployed and attached to the containers.

Enforcing mutual TLS

By default, mutual TLS is not enforced. In this section, we will enforce mutual TLS authentication step by step. We will mostly follow the steps in the following link: `https://istio.io/docs/tasks/security/authn-policy/#globally-enabling-istio-mutual-tls`.

> Please read `https://istio.io/docs/concepts/security/#authentication-policies` and `https://istio.io/docs/concepts/security/#mutual-tls-authentication` for more details.

Deploying sample services

In this example, we are using two services, `httpbin` and `sleep`, deployed under different namespaces. Two of these namespaces, `foo` and `bar`, will have the `istio` sidecar proxy. The third namespace with the `legacy` name will run the same services without the sidecar proxy.

> Make sure the Istio binaries are present in your path. `istioctl` should be runnable from the command line.

We will look at the services of namespaces by using the following commands:

1. Use the following commands to create namespaces (`foo`, `bar`, and `legacy`) and create the `httpbin` and `sleep` services in those namespaces:

```
kubectl create ns foo
kubectl apply -f <(istioctl kube-inject -f
samples/httpbin/httpbin.yaml) -n foo
kubectl apply -f <(istioctl kube-inject -f
samples/sleep/sleep.yaml) -n foo
kubectl create ns bar
kubectl apply -f <(istioctl kube-inject -f
samples/httpbin/httpbin.yaml) -n bar
```

```
kubectl apply -f <(istioctl kube-inject -f
samples/sleep/sleep.yaml) -n bar
kubectl create ns legacy
kubectl apply -f samples/httpbin/httpbin.yaml -n legacy
kubectl apply -f samples/sleep/sleep.yaml -n legacy
```

As you can see, the same services are deployed in `foo` and `bar` with the sidecar injected, while `legacy` is not.

2. Let's check whether everything is okay:

```
for from in "foo" "bar" "legacy"; do for to in "foo" "bar"
"legacy"; do kubectl exec $(kubectl get pod -l app=sleep -n ${from}
-o jsonpath={.items..metadata.name}) -c sleep -n ${from} -- curl
http://httpbin.${to}:8000/ip -s -o /dev/null -w "sleep.${from} to
httpbin.${to}: %{http_code}\n"; done; done
```

The preceding command iterates through all reachable combinations. You should see something similar to the following output:

```
sleep.foo to httpbin.foo: 200
sleep.foo to httpbin.bar: 200
sleep.foo to httpbin.legacy: 200
sleep.bar to httpbin.foo: 200
sleep.bar to httpbin.bar: 200
sleep.bar to httpbin.legacy: 200
sleep.legacy to httpbin.foo: 200
sleep.legacy to httpbin.bar: 200
sleep.legacy to httpbin.legacy: 200
```

3. Ensure that there are no existing policies, as follows:

```
kubectl get policies.authentication.istio.io --all-namespaces
No resources found.
kubectl get meshpolicies.authentication.istio.io
No resources found.
```

4. Additionally, ensure that there are no destination rules that apply:

```
kubectl get destinationrules.networking.istio.io --all-namespaces -
o yaml | grep "host:"
    host: istio-policy.istio-system.svc.cluster.local
    host: istio-telemetry.istio-system.svc.cluster.local
```

In the preceding results, there should be no hosts with `foo`, `bar`, `legacy`, or a `*` wildcard.

Globally enabling mutual TLS

Mutual TLS states that all services must use TLS when communicating with other services. This uncovers one of the big security holes in Kubernetes. A bad actor who has access to the cluster, even if they don't have access to the namespace, can send commands to any pod, pretending to be a legitimate service. If given enough rights, they can also operate as the man in the middle between services, grabbing JSON Web Tokens (JWTs). Implementing TLS between services reduces the chances of man-in-the-middle attacks between services:

1. To enable mutual TLS globally, run the following command:

```
cat <<EOF | kubectl apply -f -
apiVersion: "authentication.istio.io/v1alpha1"
kind: "MeshPolicy"
metadata:
  name: "default"
spec:
  peers:
  - mtls: {}
EOF
```

Since it is named `default`, it specifies that all workloads in the mesh will only accept encrypted requests using TLS.

2. Now run the following command:

```
for from in "foo" "bar"; do for to in "foo" "bar"; do kubectl exec
$(kubectl get pod -l app=sleep -n ${from} -o
jsonpath={.items..metadata.name}) -c sleep -n ${from} -- curl
http://httpbin.${to}:8000/ip -s -o /dev/null -w "sleep.${from} to
httpbin.${to}: %{http_code}\n"; done; done
```

Those systems with sidecars will fail when running this command and will receive a 503 code, as the client is still using plain text. It might take a few seconds for `MeshPolicy` to take effect. The following is the output:

```
sleep.foo to httpbin.foo: 503
sleep.foo to httpbin.bar: 503
sleep.bar to httpbin.foo: 503
sleep.bar to httpbin.bar: 503
```

3. We will set the destination rule to use a * wildcard that is similar to the mesh-wide authentication policy. This is required to configure the client side:

```
cat <<EOF | kubectl apply -f -
apiVersion: "networking.istio.io/v1alpha3"
kind: "DestinationRule"
```

```
metadata:
  name: "default"
  namespace: "default"
spec:
  host: "*.local"
  trafficPolicy:
    tls:
      mode: ISTIO_MUTUAL
EOF
```

Running the preceding command will make all the pods with the sidecar communicate via TLS.

4. We can check this by running the same command again:

```
for from in "foo" "bar"; do for to in "foo" "bar"; do kubectl exec
$(kubectl get pod -l app=sleep -n ${from} -o
jsonpath={.items..metadata.name}) -c sleep -n ${from} -- curl
http://httpbin.${to}:8000/ip -s -o /dev/null -w "sleep.${from} to
httpbin.${to}: %{http_code}\n"; done; done
```

This time, the returned codes will be 200:

```
sleep.foo to httpbin.foo: 200
sleep.foo to httpbin.bar: 200
sleep.bar to httpbin.foo: 200
sleep.bar to httpbin.bar: 200
```

5. We can also check that the pods without the istio sidecar cannot access any services in the foo or bar namespaces by running the following command:

```
for from in "legacy"; do for to in "foo" "bar"; do kubectl exec
$(kubectl get pod -l app=sleep -n ${from} -o
jsonpath={.items..metadata.name}) -c sleep -n ${from} -- curl
http://httpbin.${to}:8000/ip -s -o /dev/null -w "sleep.${from} to
httpbin.${to}: %{http_code}\n"; done; done
```

The result will be as follows:

```
sleep.legacy to httpbin.foo: 000
command terminated with exit code 56
sleep.legacy to httpbin.bar: 000
command terminated with exit code 56
```

Using some simple commands, we were able to dramatically increase the security of our applications without changing the application code. We achieved the goal of setting system-wide policies with operators without having developers be worried about them.

Summary

In this chapter, we learned how to secure secrets in Kubernetes. We went into detail in creating, decoding, and using secrets. We installed and injected Istio, achieving the goal of being able to set system-wide policies without needing developer intervention or oversight. Since hackers like to pick on easy systems, the skills that we have learned in this chapter will help to make your setup less likely to be targeted. In the next chapter, you will learn how to deploy serverless functions on AKS.

11
Serverless Functions

Serverless functions allow code to be deployed without worrying about managing servers and the like. In this chapter, readers will learn how to deploy serverless functions on AKS directly using Kubeless, which will be useful should they be required to provide serverless functions within their organization network. The reader will also integrate AKS-deployed applications with Azure Event Hubs. We will be covering the following topics in brief:

- Kubeless services
- Events and serverless functions

Technical requirements

You will need to use a modern browser, such as Chrome, Firefox, or Edge.

Kubeless services

The popularity of AWS Lambda, the serverless compute platform, has resulted in many frameworks that allow similar functionality, both as cloud provider-managed (for example, Azure Functions, Google Cloud Functions, and IBM Cloud Functions) and self-managed frameworks. Kubeless is one of the self-managed ones. As in any new fast-moving technology, there is no clear winner yet. Here are some open source alternatives to Kubeless that are Kubernetes friendly:

- **Serverless** (https://serverless.com/): A Node.js-based serverless application framework that can deploy and manage functions on multiple cloud providers, including Azure. Kubernetes support is provided via Kubeless.
- **OpenFaas** (https://www.openfaas.com/): A portable framework, providing ease of use for building serverless functions with Docker and Kubernetes, which has first-class support for metrics.

- **Fission.io** (https://fission.io/): A fast, open source serverless framework for Kubernetes with a focus on developer productivity and high performance.
- **Apache OpenWhisk** (https://openwhisk.apache.org/): An open source, distributed serverless platform that executes functions (fx) in response to events at any scale.
- **Knative** (https://cloud.google.com/knative/): This enables developers to focus on writing interesting code, without worrying about the difficult parts of building, deploying, and managing an application.

Kubeless was chosen based on its compatibility with the highest GitHub star winner (28K+ at the time of writing) serverless framework (https://github.com/serverless/serverless).

Installing Kubeless

This script should be pretty much expected by now. Run the following commands on Azure Cloud Shell. It will install the kubeless framework in the kubeless namespace with RBAC support:

```
helm repo add incubator
https://kubernetes-charts-incubator.storage.googleapis.com/
helm install --name kubeless  --namespace kubeless --set rbac.create=true
incubator/kubeless
```

Install Kubeless binary

While Kubeless comes up, install the Kubeless binary to launch functions in the Kubernetes cluster by running the following command:

```
export RELEASE=$(curl -s
https://api.github.com/repos/kubeless/kubeless/releases/latest | grep
tag_name | cut -d '"' -f 4)
export OS=$(uname -s| tr '[:upper:]' '[:lower:]')
curl -OL
https://github.com/kubeless/kubeless/releases/download/$RELEASE/kubeless_$O
S-amd64.zip &&   unzip kubeless_$OS-amd64.zip && mkdir -p ~/local/bin &&
mv bundles/kubeless_$OS-amd64/kubeless ~/local/bin/ && export
PATH=$PATH:~/local/bin
```

Ensure that the `kubeless` framework is installed properly by running the following command:

```
kubeless --help
```

You should get an output similar to the following:

```
Serverless framework for Kubernetes

Usage:
  kubeless [command]

Available Commands:
  autoscale          manage autoscale to function on Kubeless
  completion         Output shell completion code for the specified shell.
  function           function specific operations
  get-server-config  Print the current configuration of the controller
  help               Help about any command
  topic              manage message topics in Kubeless
  trigger            trigger specific operations
  version            Print the version of Kubeless

Flags:
  -h, --help    help for kubeless
```

Check the `helm` deploy status to ensure that everything has been installed:

```
helm status kubeless
```

You should get an output that is similar to the following:

```
LAST DEPLOYED: Sun Mar 10 04:27:03 2019
NAMESPACE: kubeless
STATUS: DEPLOYED

RESOURCES:
==> v1/ConfigMap
NAME DATA AGE
kubeless-config 8 36s

==> v1/Pod(related)
NAME READY STATUS RESTARTS AGE
kubeless-kubeless-controller-manager-5cccf45988-nc251 3/3 Running 0 36s

==> v1/ServiceAccount
NAME SECRETS AGE
controller-acct 1 36s
```

```
==> v1beta1/ClusterRole
NAME AGE
kubeless-kubeless-controller-deployer 36s

==> v1beta1/ClusterRoleBinding
NAME AGE
kafka-controller-deployer 36s
kubeless-kubeless-controller-deployer 36s

==> v1beta1/CustomResourceDefinition
NAME AGE
cronjobtriggers.kubeless.io 36s
functions.kubeless.io 36s
httptriggers.kubeless.io 36s

==> v1beta1/Deployment
NAME READY UP-TO-DATE AVAILABLE AGE
kubeless-kubeless-controller-manager 1/1 1 1 36s


NOTES:

== Deploy function

In order to deploy a function you need the kubeless binary.
You can download it from the kubeless repo:

https://github.com/kubeless/kubeless
```

Great! We are good to go to deploy our first serverless function.

The hello world serverless function

Write the following code and save it to `hello-serverless.py`:

```
# The framework is all setup to take in a
# user defined handler function (hello in this case)
# and pass data along with the event array
def hello(event, context):
    print event    return event['data']
```

Now, to deploy it, run the following code:

```
kubectl create ns serverless
kubeless function deploy hello --runtime python2.7 --from-file hello-
serverless.py --handler hello-serverless.hello -n serverless
```

Let's see what we have done in the preceding code:

- Line one: This creates a new namespace for the serverless functions.
- Line two: This deploys a serverless function named `hello` by using the `hello-serverless.py` file, with `runtime` specified as `python 2.7` and the `handler` as the `hello` function in the `serverless` namespace.

You can check whether the function is ready by running the following command:

```
kubeless function ls hello  -n serverless
```

Now, let's call it by running the following command:

```
kubeless function call hello --data 'Hello world!' -n serverless
```

You should get the following output:

```
Hello world!
```

You have successfully run your first serverless function.

Events and serverless functions

Serverless functions mainly use events to trigger their invocation. While the following invocation is useful for testing and debugging purposes, it is not really useful for other purposes. Serverless functions excel when they are run on demand and, in general, as part of some automation triggered by events. Calling them manually, as we are doing in the following code, is useful only for testing and debugging purposes:

```
kubeless function call hello --data 'Hello world!' -n serverless
```

To be really useful, we need the ability to trigger it through events. One of the easiest ways to integrate our serverless functions with events is to use Azure Event Hubs. In this section, we will integrate Azure Event Hubs with our serverless functions. We will be using Azure Functions to call our serverless function.

 There are multiple ways that a function can be linked to Event Hub. Event Grid is also an option. Please see `https://docs.microsoft.com/en-us/azure/event-grid/custom-event-quickstart` if you would like to take this route.

The following sections will cover these topics:

- How to create the Azure Function via the portal
- How to modify the code to call our serverless function

Creating and configuring Azure Functions

We have to create an Azure Function that will act as an intermediator between Azure Event Hub and our serverless function. Since Azure Functions are launched on demand, you pay for the time that they are actually used.

Perform the following steps:

1. First, create the Function App by selecting **Create a resource**, then clicking on **Compute**, then finally selecting **Function App**, as shown in the following screenshot:

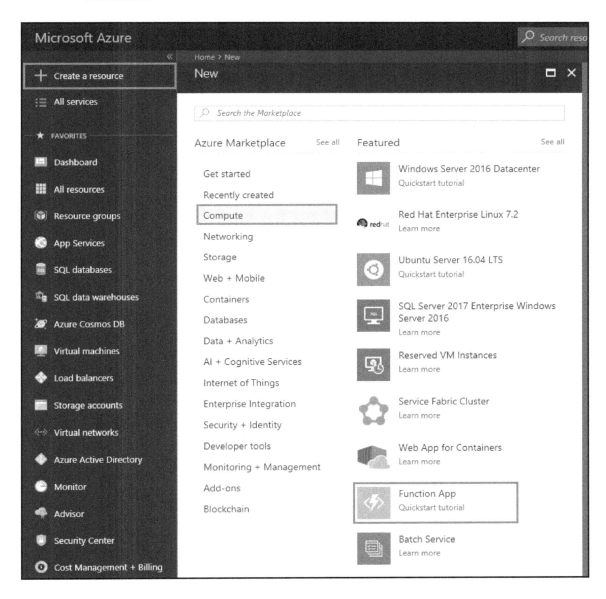

2. Now, fill in the required specifications shown in the following screenshot:

Please ensure that you select the **Windows** option and create a new **Resource Group**.

3. Since the code is in JavaScript, make sure that the **Runtime Stack** is **JavaScript**. Click on **Create**.

4. Wait for the deployment to be completed. Once it is complete, choose **Go to resource** as follows:

5. Click on **+ New Function** to add the code to call our serverless function. Choose the **In-portal** option and click on **Continue**:

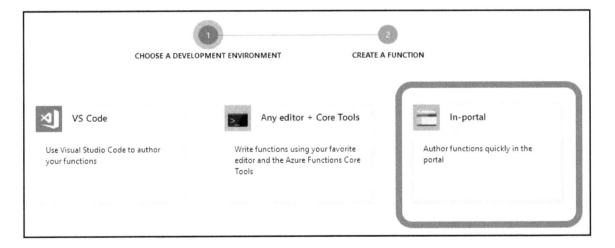

6. Choose the **More templates...** option:

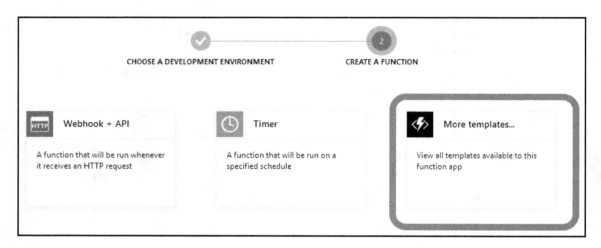

7. Click on **Finish and view templates.**
8. Select **Azure Event Hub trigger**:

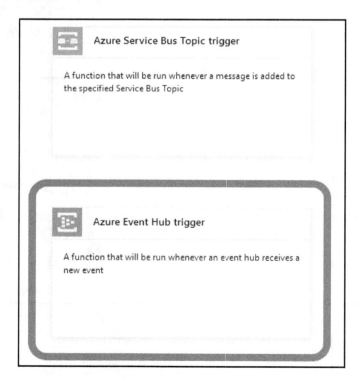

9. An **Extensions not Installed** dialog will pop up. Click on **Install**:

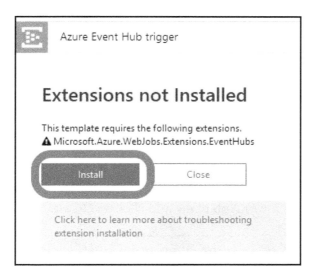

Do not close the browser while the install is going on. It can take up to two minutes. Click **Continue** once it is done.

10. In the dialog that pops up, give the function the name `UserEventHubTrigger`, and click on **new** in the **Event Hub connection** section:

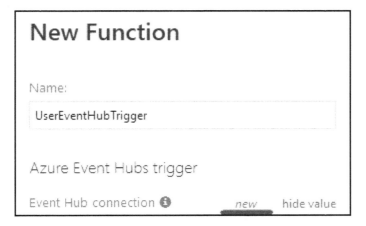

11. Select the following values:

12. Use **user** as the Event Hub name and click on **Create**:

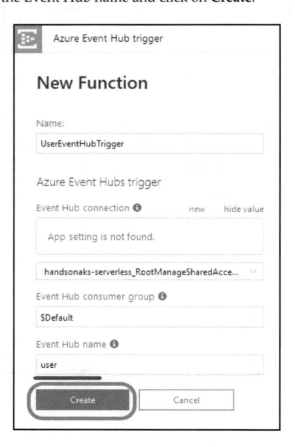

You will get the editor as follows:

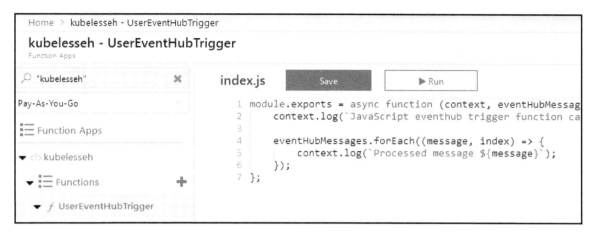

In this way, we have created and configured Azure Functions successfully.

Integrating Kubeless with Azure Event Hubs via Azure Functions

We need to expose our Kubeless function to the world so that it can be called by Azure Functions. Run the following command to expose the **hello** service:

```
kc expose --name hello-http svc/hello --type=LoadBalancer -n serverless
```

Use `kubectl get svc -n serverless` to get the `LoadBalancer` IP.

You can check whether the function works by running the following `curl` command:

```
curl -L --insecure --data '{"Hello world!"}'   --header "<Load Balancer IP"
--header "Content-Type:application/json" <Load Balancer IP>:8080
```

Now we can modify the Azure Function code whenever an event occurs in the **user** Event Hub.

Edit the function shown at the end of the previous section, as follows. Remember to replace the `LoadBalancer` IP with your value:

```
module.exports = async function (context, eventHubMessages) {
    context.log(`JavaScript eventhub trigger function called for message
array ${eventHubMessages}`);
```

```
    eventHubMessages.forEach((message, index) => {
        context.log(`Processed message ${message}`);
        const http = require('http');

        var postData = JSON.stringify({
            'msg' : 'Hello World from Event Hub!'
        });

        var options = {
        hostname: '<insert-your-kubeless-function-load-balancer-ip>', //
<<<----- IMPORTANT CHANGE THE IP HERE
        port: 8080,
        path: '',
        method: 'POST',
        headers: {
            'Content-Type': 'application/json',
            'Content-Length': postData.length
            }
        };

        var req = http.request(options, (res) => {
        console.log('statusCode:', res.statusCode);
        console.log('headers:', res.headers);

        res.on('data', (d) => {
            process.stdout.write(d);
        });
        });

        req.on('error', (e) => {
        console.error(e);
        });

        req.write(postData);
        req.end();

    });
};
```

Click on **Save and Run** once you have changed the IP address.

Your Kubeless function would have been called, and you can verify this by running the following command:

```
kc logs -f <hello-pod-name> -n serverless
```

You should see an output similar to the following:

```
10.244.3.20 - - [18/Mar/2019:08:10:17 +0000] "GET /metrics HTTP/1.1" 200
5421 "" "Prometheus/2.6.0" 0/1312
10.244.3.1 - - [18/Mar/2019:08:10:31 +0000] "GET /healthz HTTP/1.1" 200 2
"" "kube-probe/1.9" 0/102
{'event-time': None, 'extensions': {'request': <LocalRequest: POST
http://23.101.132.46:8080/>}, 'event-type': None, 'event-namespace': None,
'data': {u'msg': u'Hello World fromEvent Hub!'}, 'event-id': None}
10.244.3.1 - - [18/Mar/2019:08:10:59 +0000] "POST / HTTP/1.1" 200 38 "" ""
0/10385
```

You can verify the Event Hub integration by changing the names in **event-sourcing-microservices-example/deployment/sbin/names-15.txt** and running the following command:

```
cd event-sourcing-microservices-example && ./deployment/sbin/generate-serial.sh
```

You will see that the function is triggered in the Kubeless function logs and also in the Azure Portal, as shown in the following screenshot, by choosing the **Monitor** option:

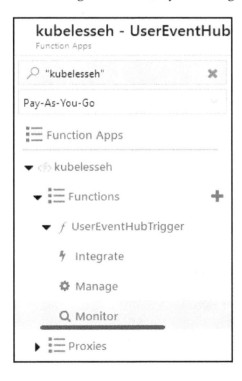

The actual log entries are shown in the following screenshot. Note that it might take couple of minutes before you see the Event Hub entries:

DATE (UTC) ⌄	SUCCESS ⌄	RESULT CODE ⌄	DURATION (MS) ⌄	OPERATION ID ⌄
2019-03-18 06:25:22.182	✓	0	10.7592	hRNo2PRjZrU=
2019-03-18 06:25:21.761	✓	0	5.3328	vl+ISVWXV18=
2019-03-18 06:25:21.403	✓	0	4.4687	FYV1miDY9ds=
2019-03-18 06:25:21.084	✓	0	10.6681	tqXlzpNS3pY=
2019-03-18 06:25:20.680	✓	0	5.5938	AXh5dIVpERA=
2019-03-18 06:25:20.249	✓	0	5.4732	b3PAb0OVzFw=
2019-03-18 06:25:19.961	✓	0	10.4079	eNh7IKWgbHY=
2019-03-18 06:25:19.028	✓	0	4.3419	AM8Hmgzyi7Q=
2019-03-18 06:25:18.717	✓	0	9.3264	U/vSxOrw5dU=
2019-03-18 06:25:18.411	✓	0	10.0801	0XbpK0/DkTl=
2019-03-18 06:25:18.021	✓	0	11.4133	LdZnQjue3uk=
2019-03-18 06:25:17.712	✓	0	10.4278	xSzSDYoDyOM=
2019-03-18 06:25:17.682	✓	0	11.1133	WHcv9j2kUGY=
2019-03-18 06:25:17.405	✓	0	68.9376	Mg8S4hGh5bs=
2019-03-18 06:20:51.963	✓	0	16.5989	BOMw5D8SsJk=
2019-03-18 06:20:13.656	✓	0	1417.6823	ENXsRG1v59Y=

Congratulations, you have successfully triggered a Kubeless serverless function using an Azure Function that, in turn, was triggered by an event that occurred in Event Hub.

Summary

This chapter was all about installing Kubeless to successfully run our first serverless function. In the latter part of the chapter, we integrated our Kubeless serverless functions with events using Azure Event Hubs. By using smaller code that is loosely coupled, we can now make faster independent releases a reality in our organization. The next and final chapter will cover future steps, where we will be pointed to different resources and can learn/implement advanced features in security and scalability. For this chapter, please refer to: https://www.packtpub.com/sites/default/files/downloads/Next_Steps.pdf

Other Books You May Enjoy

If you enjoyed this book, you may be interested in these other books by Packt:

Serverless Integration Design Patterns with Azure
Abhishek Kumar, Srinivasa Mahendrakar

ISBN: 978-1-78839-923-4

- Learn about the design principles of Microsoft Azure Serverless Integration
- Get insights into Azure Functions, Logic Apps, Azure Event Grid and Service Bus
- Secure and manage your integration endpoints using Azure API Management
- Build advanced B2B solutions using Logic Apps, Enterprise Integration Pack
- Monitor integration solutions using tools available on the market
- Discover design patterns for hybrid integration

Hands-On Azure for Developers
Kamil Mrzygłód

ISBN: 978-1-78934-062-4

- Implement serverless components such as Azure functions and logic apps
- Integrate applications with available storages and containers
- Understand messaging components, including Azure Event Hubs and Azure Queue Storage
- Gain an understanding of Application Insights and other proper monitoring solutions
- Store your data with services such as Azure SQL and Azure Data Lake Storage
- Develop fast and scalable cloud applications

Leave a review - let other readers know what you think

Please share your thoughts on this book with others by leaving a review on the site that you bought it from. If you purchased the book from Amazon, please leave us an honest review on this book's Amazon page. This is vital so that other potential readers can see and use your unbiased opinion to make purchasing decisions, we can understand what our customers think about our products, and our authors can see your feedback on the title that they have worked with Packt to create. It will only take a few minutes of your time, but is valuable to other potential customers, our authors, and Packt. Thank you!

Index